GOOD HOUSEKEEPING

Casserole Cookery

Casserole

£3.95

Book Renewals may be arranged by post	D 63751	Fines will be levied for every week or part thereof a book is overdue

This book to be returned not later than the last date on label

Return to .... $x4$ LIBRARY

Kilmarnock and Loudoun Public Libraries

GOOD HOUSEKEEPING

Cookery

GOOD HOUSEKEEPING INSTITUTE

EBURY PRESS
LONDON

Published by Ebury Press
National Magazine House
72 Broadwick Street
London W1V 2BP

First impression 1983

ISBN 0 85223 264 0 hardback
     0 85223 292 6 paperback

Designed by Harry Green
Illustrations by Vanessa Luff

Colour photography by Paul Kemp facing
pages 32, 48, 49, 97; by Paul Williams facing
page 33; by Bryce Attwell, facing page 81;
by Melvin Grey facing page 96; and by Alan
Duns facing page 80.

Jacket photograph by Paul Kemp shows
Lamb Noisettes with Pepper and Courgettes (page 34)

The publishers would like to thank Clarbat
Ltd for its help in providing casseroles by
Le Creuset and Coussances for photography.

Filmset by Advanced Filmsetters (Glasgow) Ltd
Printed and bound in Italy by New Interlitho S.p.A. Milan

Contents

Introduction

The sight of a homely earthenware casserole on the table, the rich and heady smell of gently bubbling meat and vegetables as you lift the lid – what could be more comforting on a cold winter's night? Or for summer entertaining what could be less trouble or more welcome than delicious fresh fish tenderly simmered on a bed of vegetables and herbs? All over the world there are recipes for one-pot cooking – from America's Boston Baked Beans through the meat, chicken and vegetable curries of India and the rich daubes of France to our own Lancashire Hot Pot and Irish Stew.

Whether for family meals or for lavish party occasions, for the beginner or the experienced cook, casseroles have so many advantages it is hardly surprising they have universal appeal for both cook and gourmet alike. Firstly the art of making a casserole lies not in any culinary magic, but in long, slow and gentle cooking which gives the ingredients time to blend their flavours together. There is therefore no need to use the best cuts of meat or the most expensive delicate vegetables – even the toughest meat emerges from the casserole ready to melt in the mouth. A casserole can be prepared ahead of time and, once on the hob or in the oven, it looks after itself. There is probably little or no last minute attention required and no need for a special serving dish. If you are entertaining, there need be no anxious trips to the kitchen at the eleventh hour, and it doesn't even matter if your guests are late, for as long as the heat remains low, any extra time will do no harm. Often a casserole is greatly improved by being cooked a day in advance, allowed to cool, and reheated for a short time before it is served. When you do reheat a casserole, remember to bring it to boiling point first, then simmer for 20 minutes. Casseroles freeze extremely well, so why not make two casseroles at the same time – eat one now and freeze the other for later.

All in all, casseroles are the most convenient and versatile dishes: they allow tremendous scope for inventiveness and imagination; they are generally economical, time-saving and above all undeniably delicious. They are perfect for every occasion.

TYPES OF CASSEROLES

The pot in which you cook your casserole is all important. Your type of cooker, the size of your family, your available storage space and how much cooking you do will all dictate to a certain extent which casseroles and how many you buy. Versatility is

undoubtedly the greatest asset, though there are several characteristics to be taken into consideration. The ideal casserole is the one which you can use on top of the stove or in the oven, and which also looks good enough to bring to the table. You need casseroles which won't chip or break easily, and which are simple to clean. It is certainly an advantage to have at least one which may be used safely for freezing. The cooking time and flavour of finished dishes are little affected by the material from which your casserole is made.

Heavy, cast-iron flameproof casseroles are ideal. They can be used on top of the stove or in the oven, and then brought straight to the table. They are very thick and solid and retain the heat well. They come in comforting warm colours, lined with enamel and are very hard-wearing. They can be very heavy, though, so make sure that if you are planning to buy a big one, it has two handles for easy lifting. You can brown the meat and soften the vegetables on top of the stove and move it to the oven without disturbing the ingredients, or wasting any of the precious juices. You can, of course, leave it to simmer very slowly on the top of the stove as well. China, pottery, heat-resistant glass, or the beautiful rustic earthenware pots you might have brought home from a Mediterranean holiday are ideal for casseroling, and look wonderful on the table. They could not be guaranteed to withstand an electric ring or a gas flame, so do your initial browning in a frying pan before transferring all the ingredients to the casserole for cooking. Do make sure you scrape up all the delicious residue in the bottom of the pan, as this often holds the essence of the flavour. It will help to give whatever liquid you will be using, be it water, wine, stock or beer, a quick simmer in the pan to soak up all the goodness, at the same time bringing it to the right temperature before pouring it on to the other ingredients in the casserole and putting it in the oven.

One important quality of your casserole, whatever type you have, is that it has a well-fitting lid to keep all the goodness in. The tighter the fit of the lid, the less liquid is required; and the more concentrated the natural juices, the better the flavour. If your lid does not fit properly, cover the dish first with foil, then press the lid on top for a really snug fit.

Don't forget that a tight-fitting lid can always be made of pastry, providing you seal the edges really well. There are pastry and other mouth-watering recipes for toppings at the back of the book (pages 116 to 123). Another tip is to be sure that you choose the right sized casserole for the recipe – a full pot is better than one only half full – to prevent too much evaporation.

RANGES

Lastly, do not forget that if you are lucky enough to have an Aga or any kind of kitchen range which has a constantly heated slow oven begging to be used, you could be cooking succulent casseroles every day of the week at no extra cost! Even if you have only a conventional oven you can always maximise its use by baking jacket potatoes – these are often the nicest accompaniment to the robust meat casseroles anyway – at the same time as a casserole, or use some of our vegetable casserole ideas at the same time.

CARE AND CLEANING

Once you have chosen the casserole which will best suit your requirements, it is important to take as much care of it as possible. Sensible treatment of all types of casserole will extend their lives by many years.

Don't put pots made of breakable material over direct heat unless they are marked flameproof, and never put any empty pot over direct heat while you search for the ingredients. Always use wooden or plastic spoons for stirring, and don't prod the ingredients with sharp utensils.

Whichever sort of casserole you use, as soon as it is empty and cool, the best thing to do is to soak it in warm water with a liquid detergent. Soaking for an hour or so will probably remove most of the bother of cleaning. However, you must resist the temptation to plunge hot casseroles of any sort into cold water, or to run cold water into them from the tap. This could distort metal and could easily crack glass, earthenware, pottery or porcelain, rendering them useless. Temperature shocks are the most likely causes of shortening the life of your casseroles. If you use a dishwasher, first check with the manufacturer's instructions as to whether the casserole is dishwasherproof. Most metal pots are, but beware of wooden or plastic handles.

If, after soaking and gently rubbing with a cloth, there are still stubborn patches of burnt-on food, don't try to scrape them off with sharp, pointed knives, steel wool or harsh abrasives as this will scratch and ruin the surface. A nylon scouring pad or bristle brush should be all that is needed. Stains can be removed from vitreous enamelled, cast iron casseroles by filling them with water and a little household bleach, and allowing them to soak for a while before rinsing well and wiping dry. Be careful not to immerse wooden handles in water for too long and also watch out that these do not get scorched by a neighbouring flame or ring.

Always wipe your casseroles dry before putting them away. If your storage space is limited, be careful if you have to stack earthenware, pottery or porcelain, as they will easily chip. It would, perhaps, be safer to display some of the more attractive of these pots on open shelves.

If you adhere to these few rules, your casseroles will reward you with years of service and plenty of perfectly cooked meals.

NEW-STYLE CASSEROLES

Life today often dictates that we spend less time in the kitchen. We frequently have to produce meals in a short time even if we have been out all day. However this does not mean we have to rely on convenience foods or to abandon dishes that traditionally take a long time to cook. Casseroles can be cooked in 20 minutes in a pressure cooker, will take half the usual time in a microwave oven, and can be left to cook all day without spoiling in an electric casserole.

It is vital that you follow the instructions for any of these appliances as given by the manufacturer.

Pressure Cookers

Most casserole recipes can be adapted for use in the pressure cooker. The cooking time will be reduced to about a quarter or even less of the normal cooking time. Even with the tougher cuts of meat, pressure forces steam into the meat and tenderises it very quickly. With the reduction in cooking time, and very little evaporation, less liquid is required for most recipes. Reduce the amount by up to a quarter but never use less than 300 ml ($\frac{1}{2}$ pint) of liquid. Cooking time can be reduced to between 15 minutes and 30 minutes depending on the quality, cut and size of the meat. Brown meat and vegetables in the open cooker first, then allow the pan to cool a little before adding the hot liquid. Never add thickening until the end, otherwise the thickening agent will stick and burn on the base of the cooker. The thickening agent is usually flour, which is added as a *roux*, or *beurre manié* or blended to a cream with a little cold liquid such as water. In all cases, the thickener must be thoroughly cooked in the open pressure cooker; stir or whisk while bringing to the boil.

In some recipes, all the vegetables are cooked with the meat to impart their flavour to the gravy. In other recipes some may be added towards the end of the cooking. To do this, reduce pressure, add the vegetables and then bring the cooker to pressure again for the rest of the cooking time.

Though fish cooks quickly anyway it is sometimes convenient to cut time even further by cooking it in the pressure cooker. Many vegetables can be cooked in the same amount of time. If your pressure cooker is large enough, put the fish in an ovenproof or flameproof casserole that will fit the cooker, together with the vegetables and flavourings and cook according to the recipe. Many pulse recipes are also ideal for the pressure cooker, but remember they must be soaked for at least 12 hours first, as for normal casserole cooking.

A pressure cooker is particularly useful for making bulk quantities of stews and casseroles for storing in the freezer. Whatever the quantity made, it still requires the same cooking time, but remember that the pressure cooker must never be more than three-quarters full.

Microwave Ovens

These can also be useful for making casseroles quickly – cooking times can be reduced by about a half, and produce very successful results. As with a conventional oven however, they are better prepared a day in advance and gently reheated when required. In order to keep the cooking rate slow, to allow time for tougher meat fibres to tenderise, casseroles using cheaper cuts of meat should be cooked on a low power setting.

Cut meat and vegetables into pieces of roughly the same size to ensure even cooking. Sauté the meat and vegetables separately either in the browning dish in the microwave, or in a frying pan on the stove, then combine the two. You may find you can reduce the liquid required by about a third, as there is little evaporation in microwave cooking. Casseroles should be covered, and stirred during the cooking time to ensure that the uppermost and outer pieces of meat do not become dry. If casseroles are cooked in a small amount of liquid be careful to stir, and scrape the edges to prevent sauces becoming lumpy or congealed against the sides of the dish. Standing time is essential for all meats whether joints or casseroles, and it helps to tenderise them further. Follow the manufacturer's instructions for the length of standing time. Microwaves are also useful for reheating small amounts of frozen casseroles. Freeze the food in a container suitable for use in the microwave so it can be defrosted, heated or cooked straight from the freezer.

Electric Casseroles

An electric casserole provides a modern method of slow cooking without using a conventional oven. It will save up to two-thirds of the fuel which would be used in a conventional oven. It is really an updated hay-box, heating the food inside the casserole evenly and slowly because it is totally surrounded by heat. The cooking pot is usually earthenware to ensure even distribution of heat. A low setting point allows the food to cook for up to twelve hours without burning or sticking.

Meat and vegetables should both be browned in a separate pan before being put in the electric casserole. Boiling liquid should then be poured on. The food is heated to a temperature high enough to destroy harmful bacteria and ensure that the correct temperature is maintained throughout the cooking time. Don't be tempted to lift the lid during cooking time as the temperature will drop and may take a long time to be regained. If you have to add vegetables, dumplings or other toppings near the end of cooking time, turn the temperature control to high and leave the lid off for as short a time as possible.

As most vegetables have such a dense composition they can take longer to cook than meat in these cookers. They must therefore be cut quite small. Some vegetables that you would not normally add to a casserole until near the end of cooking time because they would overcook can be added to the electric casserole at the beginning; cauliflower florets, sliced courgettes, mushrooms, for example will keep their shape and colour. Frozen vegetables should be completely defrosted before being added to the electric casserole; if they are added while still frozen the temperature drops drastically and you run the risk of bacteria multiplying. Dried beans, peas and pulses must be soaked for 12 hours and drained before adding to the casserole. With pulses, and kidney beans in particular, it is very important to bring to the boil and boil for 10 minutes before adding to the casserole. Alternatively use a can of beans instead and add it straight to the pan.

All fat should be removed from meat as the low cooking temperature will only reduce it to a soft unpleasant texture instead of melting it. All frozen meat and poultry must be completely thawed before cooking. All stock or cooking liquid must be brought to the boil before adding to the other ingredients in the casserole. This hastens the time taken for the 'safe temperature' to be reached.

Meat or vegetables can be tossed in seasoned flour before cooking, or it is possible to thicken sauces or gravies at the end of the process, by blending cornflour with a little cold water and stirring it into the casserole. If the dish has been cooked on the high setting, the cornflour will thicken immediately. If the dish has been cooked on the low setting, the lid may need to be replaced and cooking continued for about 10–15 minutes, until the sauce thickens.

Though food cooked in the electric casserole is ideal for freezing, never reheat cooked frozen food in the casserole. The low cooking temperature cannot heat the food fast enough for it to be safe.

FREEZING

Casseroles freeze beautifully and are quite as good as when freshly cooked, so it is always well worth working on the 'eat some, keep some' system, so that there is always a main dish in reserve.

There are no hard and fast rules for storage times but prolonged storage will cause flavours to deteriorate.

Before freezing any casserole check the recipe to make sure that it is suitable for freezing, and take into account any specific instructions in the recipe. Remember these points:

- For long-term storage, use seasonings sparingly. Reduce onion and garlic too, as their flavours change if they are frozen for more than a month. Check and adjust seasoning before serving.
- Cool the cooked casserole as quickly as possible. This can be done by standing the pot in cold or iced water, stirring occasionally. Skim off excess fat.
- Liquid expands on freezing, so leave 1 cm ($\frac{1}{2}$ inch) head space at the top.
- Freeze units of around 1 litre (2 pints): these are easier to reheat than very large packs.

Packing for the Freezer

There are several different ways of packing a casserole. You can freeze it in the dish in which it was cooked, but remember the dish will then be out of service for a while. If your casserole has straight sides and no lips, turn the cool mixture out and wash the casserole. Return the original contents and freeze until solid. Then dip the dish in hot water for a brief moment, slip out the solid block and wrap well in foil or a polythene freezer bag. Yet another way is to foil-line a clean casserole, leaving a good margin for wrapping over, and spoon in the cool contents. Once frozen solid, slip out the block and fold the foil over. Place inside a polythene bag and secure.

If you don't want to have the casserole out of commission in the freezer, line any rigid container or dish with freezer foil or a freezer bag and fill with the cooled, cooked casserole. If using foil, cut enough to completely overwrap the casserole. Freeze in the normal way, remove the casserole from the container, and overwrap or secure the top of the bag. Another way is to turn the cooled mixture into a rigid foil and lidded container. The food can then be reheated later and transferred to a serving dish for the table.

Always label and date everything you put in the freezer, and keep a note of what has been frozen when. Eat the food in rotation, so you don't keep some casseroles longer than others.

Reheating

Casseroles are best thawed before reheating, but they can be cooked from frozen. Thaw at room temperature for about eight hours or overnight.

It is important to bring the casserole to the boil when reheating, and this is done by either of two methods:

(1) on top of the stove in a saucepan or flameproof casserole, and then simmer for 20 minutes.
(2) in the oven in a covered casserole at 220°C (425°F) mark 7. A medium-sized casserole will take about 30 minutes to reach boiling point and should then be cooked for a further 20 minutes at 150°C (300°F) mark 2.

If reheating a casserole straight from the freezer, unwrap the preformed casserole and heat it gently in a heavy based saucepan, stirring occasionally so it does not stick. Don't try to hurry it along too much or stir too often as this will only break down the ingredients and destroy the appearance of the casserole. Bring to the boil when thawed, then simmer for 20 minutes.

It is possible to add cobbler, dumpling, and other toppings after reheating a frozen casserole. Cook as in the original recipe.

Meat

The versatility of meat casseroles is such that some form of rich, meaty hotpot is probably to be found on the tables of most households at least once a week. Inexperienced cooks may often hesitate to buy less familiar cuts of meat, and yet these are often cheaper and much better value than for example chops, cutlets or steaks — all they require is the simple treatment of a casserole, and they produce wonderfully economical, nutritious and above all, delicious meals. Most of the cheaper cuts of meat are tastier than the more expensive ones, and yet they are usually on the tough side. If they are cooked quickly, as one would cook a steak or chop, they dry out and become tougher still. What they need is long, slow cooking in liquid, in a covered pot to keep their tasty juices intact and to tenderise the meat.

The best way to cook casseroles is to start by drying the meat and vegetables before the initial frying. If you want a thick sauce, toss the cut meat in seasoned flour first — do this at the last minute otherwise the meat juices will be drawn out into the flour which will become sticky and lumpy. With any initial frying don't overcrowd the pan or the ingredients will 'stew'. Brown the meat or poultry a little at a time, transferring each piece to the casserole as you go, or putting it aside until all is done. Browning both seals the flavour into the meat, and helps give the eventual gravy a rich brown colour. Quickly fry any vegetables in the hot fat before transferring them to the casserole along with the meat. If you prefer your vegetables crisp, it is better to add them later so that they don't cook so long. Add the liquid, bring to the boil, then reduce it to a simmer for cooking on top of the stove, or set the oven heat to a low temperature to keep the pot at simmering point.

If you find that your gravy is too thin, then you can always thicken it by adding cornflour blended with a little water, or drain the gravy and reduce it by boiling fast in another pan. If on the other hand your problem is too much oil or unappetising grease — and this can happen with some of the fattier cuts of meat — either cool the casserole and remove the solidified fat, or gently drag a piece of absorbent kitchen paper across the surface, or even try dropping ice cubes into the strained liquid — the fat will congeal round the cubes — but remove them before they have a chance to melt.

If you are using wine or cider in your casserole, and even the merest drop makes a huge difference, you can marinate the meat overnight in the wine with some herbs and perhaps oil or vegetables so that the flavour soaks right in. Cook the meat in the strained juices of the marinade. Not only does this improve the flavour of the meat, it also helps to tenderise it.

Beef

Beef seems such a robust rich meat that it is often the first choice when one wants a substantial meal. The more economical cuts of beef, which can certainly be tougher but are often tastier than prime cuts, like flank, leg, shin, chuck, skirt or blade, are ideal for casseroling. While it is obviously best to avoid very fatty pieces of meat, do not go for pieces of meat with no fat, since this will keep it moist during cooking and also add to the flavour. Fat on meat should be firm and free from dark marks or discolouration.

The colour and texture of beef are so rich they demand a suitably respectful treatment. Good, strong flavours penetrate beef very satisfactorily, from the aromatic spices of the oriental recipes to the wine or beer of the sumptuous beef classics, Boeuf Bourguignonne or Carbonade.

Braised Beef

1.4 kg (3 lb) joint silverside of beef

225 g (8 oz) parsnips, peeled and thickly sliced

225 g (8 oz) turnip, peeled and chopped

225 g (8 oz) carrots, peeled and thickly sliced

225 g (8 oz) onion, skinned and sliced

225 g (8 oz) celery, washed and sliced

75 g (3 oz) streaky bacon rashers

25 g (1 oz) lard or dripping

150 ml (¼ pint) beef stock

150 ml (¼ pint) cider

salt and freshly ground pepper

bayleaf

15 ml (3 level tsp) arrowroot

SERVES 4–6

Tie up the meat to form a neat joint. Mix the sliced vegetables together. This is known as a *mirepoix* and gives flavour to the meat.

Melt the lard or dripping in a 3.4-litre (6-pint) deep flameproof casserole. Lay the rashers on the base and heat gently until the bacon fat runs, increase heat slightly and fry until bacon begins to brown. Take casserole off heat, lift out bacon with a draining spoon, cool. Snip off rind and divide each rasher into 3 or 4 pieces.

Reheat the fat in the casserole for a few seconds. Brown the meat all over, turning it with long handled spoons. If the fat is not hot enough the meat will not seal quickly and its juices will run into the fat, lowering the temperature and preventing the meat from browning properly. When browned evenly remove from casserole.

Add the vegetables to the pan and fry over a high heat until tinged with colour, stir frequently to prevent pieces burning on to the base of the pan. Stir the bacon pieces, seasonings and bayleaf through the vegetables and season well. Place the joint in the centre of the bed of vegetables.

Pour the hot stock and cider into the casserole. The liquid should barely cover the vegetables. Bring to the boil and remove from the heat. Fit a piece of kitchen foil over the meat and vegetables to form a 'tent'. Cover the dish with a close fitting lid to prevent the steam from escaping.

Cook in the oven at 160–170°C (300–325°F) mark 2–3 for 2–2½ hours. Halfway through the cooking time turn the joint over and re-cover firmly. After 2 hours test the meat – if done a fine skewer will glide easily and smoothly into the joint.

Lift the joint on to a board and cut into slices no more than 5 mm (¼ inch) thick. Remove the vegetables from the casserole with two draining spoons. Let all the cooking liquor run back into the pan. Discard the bayleaf and place the vegetables on a shallow serving dish, arrange the meat across the top, cover with foil and keep warm in a low oven.

Mix the arrowroot to a smooth thin paste with 45 ml (3 tbsp) water. Skim off excess fat from the juices. Off the heat stir the paste into the juices then bring slowly to boil, stirring. Bubble for 1 minute and adjust seasoning. Spoon a little gravy over meat, sprinkle with a little snipped parsley. Serve the rest of the gravy separately.

Not suitable for freezing.

VARIATION

Place the prepared vegetables in a deep bowl, pour over 300 ml (½ pint) red wine and 30 ml (2 tbsp) vegetable oil. Add a large clove of garlic, skinned and crushed, and a bayleaf. Season well. Push the 1.4 kg (3 lb) joint silverside down among the vegetables. Cover tightly with cling film and leave in a cool place for 6–8 hours, turning once or twice and basting with the wine.

Remove meat from marinade, pat dry. Drain vegetables, reserving marinade. Fry bacon, meat and vegetables as in basic recipe. Continue cooking but use strained marinade in place of the stock and cider.

Cottage Pie with Ale

450 g (1 lb) lean minced beef	1 small garlic clove, skinned and crushed	salt and freshly ground pepper
50 g (2 oz) butter or margarine	30 ml (2 level tbsp) plain flour	900 g (2 lb) potatoes, peeled
2 medium onions, skinned and thinly sliced	300 ml (½ pint) beef stock	30 ml (2 level tbsp) French mustard
10 ml (2 level tsp) demerara sugar	150 ml (¼ pint) brown ale	1 egg, beaten
	2 bayleaves	

SERVES 4

Brown the meat well in a saucepan. Remove with a slotted spoon. Melt 25 g (1 oz) fat and brown the onion with the sugar, and then add the garlic. Stir in the plain flour and cook for 2 minutes before adding the stock, ale and bayleaves. Replace the meat and season. Bring it to the boil, cover and simmer for 1 hour. Skim the fat off if necessary.

Boil the potatoes in salted water. Drain and mash them, then cream with the mustard, egg and remaining fat. Spoon the meat juices into a shallow ovenproof dish. Spoon or pipe the mashed potato on top.

Brown in the oven at 190°C (375°F) mark 5 for 30 minutes.

Suitable for freezing. Reheat in the usual way.

Boiled Beef and Carrots with Herb Dumplings

1.8-kg (4-lb) piece of fresh
   salted brisket or silverside
30 ml (2 level tsp) salt per
   450 g (1 lb) meat
bouquet garni
3—4 onions, skinned and left
   whole

4—6 small carrots, peeled and
   left whole or sliced
2—3 leeks, or 1—2 sticks of
   celery, cleaned and cut in
   5-cm (2-inch) lengths
1 small turnip, peeled and
   quartered

For the dumplings
100 g (4 oz) self-raising flour
salt
2.5 ml ($\frac{1}{2}$ level tsp) mixed
   dried herbs
50 g (2 oz) shredded suet

SERVES 6

To calculate the cooking time, allow 30 minutes per 450 g (1 lb) and 30 minutes over for meat up to 1.4 kg (3 lb); 45 minutes per 450 g (1 lb) for joints any larger than this — ie 3 hours for a 1.8-kg (4-lb) piece. Put it in a large pan with the salt and enough water to cover, bring slowly to the boil, skim off any scum that rises, add the bouquet garni, cover with a lid, reduce the heat and leave to simmer. Three-quarters of an hour before the cooking is complete, add the vegetables and continue cooking.

To make the dumplings, combine all the ingredients and bind with water to give an elastic dough; divide into 10—12 small pieces and roll into balls. Add to the pan about $\frac{1}{4}$ hour before cooking is complete, cover and simmer for 15—20 minutes, or until the dumplings swell and rise to the top of the pan. If the pan is rather full, pour off some of the cooking liquid into a separate pan, bring this to the boil, drop in the dumplings and cook as above. Remove the bouquet garni and serve the meat hot, surrounded by the vegetables and dumplings. Any meat left over is excellent used cold for sandwiches or served with salad.

Salted brisket, silverside or belly of pork can also be cooked in this way. If very salty, soak for 3—4 hours before cooking, rinse, then cover with fresh water and proceed as for unsalted meat, but allow 1 hour per 450 g (1 lb) for joints up to 1.4 kg (3 lb) and 3—4 hours for joints weighing 1.8—2.3 kg (4—5 lb).

Not suitable for freezing.

Beef and Venison in Red Wine

900 g (2 lb) shin of beef
450 g (1 lb) stewing venison
175 g (6 oz) onion, skinned
and sliced
300 ml (½ pint) dry red wine
15 ml (1 level tbsp) coriander
seeds

2 bayleaves
350 g (12 oz) celery
350 g (12 oz) mushrooms,
wiped and sliced
60 ml (4 tbsp) vegetable oil
30 ml (2 level tbsp) flour

450 ml (¾ pint) beef stock
salt and freshly ground
pepper
1 garlic clove, skinned and
crushed
parsley, snipped, to garnish

SERVES 8

Cut the beef into strips and the venison into chunks. Add the wine, coriander seeds and bayleaves. Marinate in a cool place for 24 hours turning occasionally.

Strain off the marinade and reserve it, discarding the bayleaves. Slice the celery into 7.5-cm (3-inch) lengths. Heat the oil in a large flameproof casserole, brown the meat and onions in batches. Remove and add the celery and mushrooms and brown them quickly. Sprinkle flour over the vegetables; add the stock, seasoning, marinade and garlic; bring to the boil and replace the meat and onion.

Cover the casserole and cook in the oven at 150°C (300°F) mark 2 for about 3 hours or until tender. Garnish with snipped parsley. Serve with redcurrant jelly.

Suitable for freezing. Reheat in the usual way.

Beef and Dumpling Ragout

900 g (2 lb) lean stewing
beef, cubed
45 ml (3 tbsp) vegetable oil
50 g (2 oz) butter
450 g (1 lb) parsnips, peeled
and cut into chunks
60 ml (4 level tbsp) flour

450 g (1 lb) onions, skinned
and quartered
30 ml (2 level tbsp) tomato
purée
1 litre (1¾ pint) beef stock
salt and freshly ground
pepper

125 g (4 oz) streaky bacon
rashers, rinded
175 g (6 oz) self-raising flour
75 g (3 oz) shredded suet
45 ml (3 tbsp) chopped
parsley

SERVES 6

Seal the meat in hot oil and butter in a large flameproof casserole. Drain the meat from the fat and set aside.

Lightly brown the parsnips and onions in the fat. Stir in 60 ml (4 level tbsp) flour, fry for a few minutes, add the tomato purée, stock and seasoning. Bring to the boil, return the meat and cover tightly. Transfer to the oven and cook at 170°C (325°F) mark 3 about 1¾ hours. Skim well.

Meanwhile grill the bacon and snip into small pieces. Mix with self-raising flour, suet, parsley and seasoning and bind it together with cold water to form a soft dough. Shape it into twelve small balls, and drop them on to the stew. Cover with a tight-fitting lid and return to the oven for further 30–40 minutes. Serve really hot.

Suitable for freezing. Freeze without the dumplings. Reheat in the usual way, add dumplings and finish as above.

Beef Paupiettes with Port

Choose a wide shallow flameproof casserole for this dish, ideally one that can go on the table. The beef needs to cook in a single layer at a steady heat for the best results.

50 g (2 oz) brown rice
25 g (1 oz) unsalted peanuts
75 g (3 oz) mushrooms, chopped
50 g (2 oz) butter
1 egg, size 6

45 ml (3 tbsp) chopped parsley
salt and freshly ground pepper
six 125-g (4-oz) thin slices of beef topside

45 ml (3 tbsp) vegetable oil
350 g (12 oz) onion, skinned and sliced
150 ml ($\frac{1}{4}$ pint) port
snipped parsley to garnish

SERVES 6

Cook the rice in plenty of boiling salted water for about 30 minutes until just tender, and drain well. Finely chop the unsalted peanuts. Heat the butter in a medium sized frying pan and sauté the mushrooms and peanuts, turning frequently until any excess moisture has evaporated. Remove from the heat and mix in the cooked rice, parsley and egg, season well. Trim the slices of topside and bat out between sheets of greaseproof or non-stick paper. Place a spoonful of the rice mixture on each piece of meat and tie up into neat parcels. Heat the oil in a shallow flameproof casserole and nicely brown the paupiettes all over. Take them out of the pan and add the onions and lightly brown. Replace the paupiettes in a single layer and pour in the port. Season and bring to the boil. Cover the dish tightly and cook in the oven at 170°C (325°F) mark 3 for about 1 hour. Remove the string for serving and sprinkle the dish generously with snipped parsley.

Suitable for freezing. Reheat in the usual way.

Braised Beef with Lentils

salt and freshly ground pepper
450 g (1 lb) lean minced beef
15 ml (1 tbsp) vegetable oil
2 medium onions, skinned and sliced

1.25 ml ($\frac{1}{4}$ level tsp) chilli powder
175 g (6 oz) red lentils
45 ml (3 tbsp) soy sauce
5 ml (1 tsp) Worcestershire sauce

15 ml (1 level tbsp) yeast extract
226-g (8-oz) can tomatoes
chopped spring onion or snipped parsley to garnish

SERVES 4

Season the minced beef and shape into eight patties. Heat the oil in a flameproof casserole and brown the patties well on both sides. Remove with a slotted spoon. In the same pan brown the onion, then stir in the chilli powder. Cook for 2 minutes before stirring in all the remaining ingredients, except the garnish, with 600 ml (1 pint) water. Bring to the boil, cover and simmer for 30 minutes. Place the patties on the lentil mixture, cover and finish cooking in the oven at 180°C (350°F) mark 4 for a further 30 minutes. If necessary skim fat off. Serve sprinkled with chopped spring onion or snipped parsley.

Not suitable for freezing.

Beef and Vegetable Casserole

450 g (1 lb) shin of beef, trimmed and cubed

15 ml (1 level tbsp) seasoned flour

30 ml (2 tbsp) vegetable oil

75 g (3 oz) celery, washed and sliced

75 g (3 oz) carrots, peeled and sliced

125 g (4 oz) onion, skinned and sliced

1 garlic clove, skinned and crushed

175 g (6 oz) tomatoes, skinned, seeded and roughly chopped

6 black olives, halved and stoned

1.25 ml ($\frac{1}{4}$ level tsp) dried oregano

salt and freshly ground pepper

75 ml (5 tbsp) red wine, dry cider or light beer

200 ml (7 fl oz) beef stock

SERVES 4

Toss the beef in the seasoned flour and brown well in hot oil in a flameproof casserole. Remove from the casserole using a slotted spoon. Add the celery, carrots and onion to the residual fat in the pan and fry until lightly coloured. Add the garlic. Return the meat to the casserole with the tomatoes, olives and oregano. Pour over the wine, cider or beer and the stock. Add seasoning to taste. Cook in the oven, covered, at 170°C (325°F) mark 3 for about 2 hours or until the meat is tender.

Serve plain or with one of the toppings on pages 117–119.

Suitable for freezing. Reheat in the usual way.

Oriental Meatballs

50 g (2 oz) butter or margarine

1 medium onion, skinned and finely chopped

450 g (1 lb) minced beef

50 g (2 oz) fresh brown breadcrumbs

5 ml (1 tsp) Worcestershire sauce

1 egg

salt and freshly ground pepper

45 ml (3 tbsp) vegetable oil

1 medium green pepper, seeded and roughly chopped

1 medium red pepper, seeded and roughly chopped

30 ml (2 level tbsp) soft brown sugar

10 ml (2 tsp) soy sauce

30 ml (2 tbsp) vinegar

150 ml ($\frac{1}{4}$ pint) orange juice

150 ml ($\frac{1}{4}$ pint) beef stock

15 ml (1 level tbsp) cornflour

SERVES 4

Heat the fat in a pan, add the onion and cook for about 5 minutes until softened. Stir in the mince, breadcrumbs, Worcestershire sauce and egg and season well.

Use damp hands to shape the mixture into twelve balls. Chill for 20 minutes. In a large frying pan brown the meatballs well in the hot oil. Remove with a slotted spoon. Add the peppers and sauté for 2 minutes. Stir in the sugar, soy sauce, vinegar, orange juice, stock and seasoning. Bring to the boil and replace meatballs. Cover and cook in the oven at 180°C (350°F) mark 4 for about 45 minutes. Skim if necessary. Drain the cooking liquor from the meatballs, keep them warm in a serving dish. Mix the cornflour to a smooth paste with a little water; stir into pan juices. Bring to the boil and cook stirring for 2–3 minutes, pour over the meatballs.

Not suitable for freezing.

Casseroled Spiced Beef

15 ml (1 tbsp) vegetable oil
125 g (4 oz) onion, skinned
 and sliced
125 g (4 oz) celery, sliced
1 garlic clove, skinned and
 crushed
50 g (2 oz) lean streaky
 bacon, diced
450 g (1 lb) lean minced beef

15 ml (1 level tbsp) flour
30 ml (2 level tbsp) curry
 powder
2.5 ml (½ level tsp) ground
 ginger
5 ml (1 level tsp) tomato
 purée
150 ml (¼ pint) natural
 yogurt

salt and freshly ground
 pepper
225 g (8 oz) tomatoes,
 skinned, quartered, seeded
250 g (8 oz) cucumber
50 g (2 oz) butter
25 g (1 oz) split blanched
 almonds

SERVES 4

Heat the oil and fry the onion and the celery until they are lightly browned. Add the garlic and bacon and cook for 2 minutes. Stir in the mince and brown it all over, stirring to break up the mince. Blend in the flour, curry powder, ginger, tomato purée and yogurt. Season well. Bring to the boil and stir in the tomatoes. Transfer everything to a casserole and bake in the oven at 190°C (375°F) mark 5 for about 45 minutes.

Slice the cucumber into thick matchsticks and sauté in butter for 2 minutes. Season and stir it through the beef. Top with almonds fried in butter and sprinkled with paprika. Serve hot with oven fresh herb bread.

Suitable for freezing. Freeze without cucumber and almonds. Reheat in the usual way, add cucumber and almonds.

Goulash

700 g (1½ lb) stewing steak,
 cut into 1-cm (½-inch) cubes
45 ml (3 level tbsp) seasoned
 flour
2 medium onions, skinned
 and chopped
1 green pepper, seeded and
 chopped

30 ml (2 tbsp) fat or
 vegetable oil
10 ml (2 level tsp) paprika
45 ml (3 level tbsp) tomato
 purée
little grated nutmeg
salt and freshly ground
 pepper

50 g (2 oz) flour
300 ml (½ pint) beef stock
2 large tomatoes, skinned
 and quartered
bouquet garni
150 ml (¼ pint) beer

SERVES 4

Coat the meat with seasoned flour. Fry the onions and pepper lightly in the fat or oil for about 3–4 minutes. Add the meat and fry lightly on all sides until golden brown – about 5 minutes. Add the paprika and fry for about a minute longer. Stir in the tomato purée, nutmeg, seasoning and flour and cook for a further 2–3 minutes. Add the stock, tomatoes and bouquet garni, put into a casserole and cook in the oven at 170°C (325°F) mark 3 for 1½–2 hours. Add the beer, cook for a few minutes longer and remove the bouquet garni. Serve with boiled noodles, sauerkraut and dumplings (see page 121), or with a green salad.

Suitable for freezing. Reheat in the usual way.

Steak and Kidney Pie

700 g (1½ lb) stewing steak
225 g (8 oz) ox kidney
25 g (1 oz) seasoned flour
1 medium onion, skinned
and sliced
25 g (1 oz) lard

225 g (8 oz) button
mushrooms
150 ml (¼ pint) beef stock
30 ml (2 level tbsp) tomato
ketchup

45 ml (3 tbsp) chopped
parsley
368-g (13-oz) packet frozen
puff pastry, thawed
beaten egg

SERVES 6

Cut the steak and kidney into cubes; toss in seasoned flour. Over a high heat fry the onion, meats and mushrooms in the lard. Add the stock, ketchup and parsley, bring to the boil and season. Place a pie funnel in the centre of a 1.1-litre (2-pint) pie dish. Fill with the meat mixture and allow it to cool.

Roll out the pastry and cover the pie, decorating it with pastry trimmings. Glaze with beaten egg. Bake in the oven at 230°C (450°F) mark 8 for 20 minutes. Cover loosely with foil; reduce heat to 180°C (350°F) mark 4 for a further 2 hours.

Suitable for freezing. Freeze the pie uncooked. Thaw at cool, room temperature overnight and cook as above.

Beef in Brandy and Mustard

Select a piece of chuck steak that's compact in shape. Chill it for about ½ hour in the freezer to make slicing easier.

1.1 kg (2½ lb) chuck steak in
a piece
1 medium onion, skinned and
sliced
30 ml (2 tbsp) vegetable oil
50 g (2 oz) butter

60 ml (4 tbsp) brandy
1 garlic clove, skinned and
crushed
15 ml (1 level tbsp) whole
grain mustard
300 ml (½ pint) beef stock

salt and freshly ground
pepper
225 g (8 oz) tender crisp
celery, trimmed
50 g (2 oz) walnut halves
75 ml (5 tbsp) single cream

SERVES 6 ——— *Illustrated in colour opposite page 32*

Cut the chuck steak into thin strips, discarding excess fat. Heat the oil together with 25 g (1 oz) butter in a medium-sized flameproof casserole and brown the meat well, a little at a time; take out and drain. Add the onion to the reheated pan juices and fry until golden; return the meat to the casserole and flame with the brandy. Stir in the garlic with the mustard, stock and seasoning and bring to the boil. Cover the dish tightly and cook in the oven at 150°C (300°F) mark 2 for about 1½ hours or until the meat is quite tender.

Meanwhile, cut the celery diagonally into fine strips and, just before serving time, sauté with the walnuts in the remaining butter until golden. Add the cream and walnut mixture to the meat and bring to the boil, stirring, simmer for 2–3 minutes. Adjust seasoning and serve at once.

Suitable for freezing. Freeze without celery, walnuts and cream. Reheat in the usual way, add celery, walnuts and cream.

Brewers' Braise

100 g (4 oz) stoned prunes
700 g (1½ lb) stewing beef
30 ml (2 tbsp) vegetable oil
2 large onions, skinned and
  sliced
15 ml (1 level tbsp) flour

275-ml (9.68-fl oz) can of
  beer
298-ml (10½-oz) can of
  condensed cream of
  tomato soup

225 g (8 oz) carrots, peeled
  and sliced
salt and freshly ground
  pepper
croûtons

SERVES 4

Cover prunes with boiling water and leave to stand for 30 minutes. Drain. Cut the meat into fork size pieces. Brown well in the oil in a flameproof casserole. Remove with a slotted spoon. Add the onions to the residual oil and lightly brown. Stir in the flour and cook for 1 minute. Stir in the beer, the soup (undiluted), the prunes and carrots. Bring to the boil and season well. Replace the meat, cover and cook in the oven at 170°C (325°F) mark 3 for 1½–2 hours until tender.

Serve garnished with croûtons.

Suitable for freezing. Reheat in the usual way.

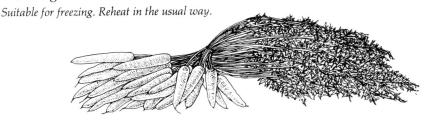

Pot-au-Feu

This is a classic French dish. Traditionally, the meat should be sliced and served with the vegetables. Serve the broth, sprinkled with parsley as a starter.

1 kg (2¼ lb) lean beef (brisket,
  flank or topside)
salt and freshly ground
  pepper
1 carrot, peeled and
  quartered
1 turnip, peeled and
  quartered

3 litres (5¼ pints) water
1 onion, skinned and
  quartered
1 parsnip, peeled and
  quartered
2 small leeks, quartered and
  washed

2 stalks of celery, trimmed
  and quartered
1 small cabbage, washed and
  halved
bouquet garni
30 ml (2 level tbsp) seed pearl
  tapioca

SERVES 4

Tie the meat securely to keep it in one piece, put into a large saucepan, add the water and 10 ml (2 level tsp) salt, cover and simmer for 2 hours. Add the vegetables (except the cabbage) and the bouquet garni and cook for another 2 hours. Put the cabbage into the pan and continue cooking for a final 30 minutes, or until it is soft. Strain off most of the liquid, put into a pan, bring to the boil, sprinkle in the tapioca and simmer for about 15 minutes, or until the tapioca clears. Adjust seasoning before serving.

Not suitable for freezing.

Beef Olives

75 g (3 oz) streaky bacon, rinded and finely chopped	1.25 ml (¼ level tsp) dried mixed herbs	1 egg, size 6
1 small onion, skinned and chopped	1 lemon	15 ml (1 level tbsp) made English mustard
10 ml (2 tsp) chopped parsley	salt and freshly ground pepper	45 ml (3 level tbsp) seasoned flour
125 g (4 oz) fresh breadcrumbs	8 thin slices of beef topside, about 700 g (1½ lb) total weight	60 ml (4 tbsp) vegetable oil
50 g (2 oz) shredded suet		400 ml (¾ pint) beef stock
		225 g (8 oz) onions, skinned

SERVES 4

In a bowl, mix together the bacon, onion, parsley, breadcrumbs, suet and herbs. Add the grated rind of ½ lemon, 5 ml (1 tsp) juice, seasoning and egg.

Trim the meat and bat out the slices between sheets of cling film. Spread the mustard thinly over meat. Divide the stuffing equally between the pieces. Roll them up and secure them with fine string. Toss each one in seasoned flour.

Heat the oil in a shallow flameproof casserole into which the beef olives will just fit. Brown them well and remove them from the fat. Stir the remaining seasoned flour into the pan residue and brown lightly. Gradually add the stock and bring to the boil. Season and replace the meat.

Slice the onions into rings and scatter them over the meat. Cover and cook in the oven at 170°C (325°F) mark 3 for about 1½ hours.

Suitable for freezing. Reheat in the usual way.

Marinated Spiced Beef with Rice

142 ml (5 fl oz) soured cream	5 ml (1 level tsp) turmeric	225 g (8 oz) long grain rice
1 garlic clove, skinned and crushed	5 ml (1 level tsp) coriander	30 ml (2 tbsp) chopped parsley
30 ml (2 level tbsp) tomato purée	5 ml (1 level tsp) curry powder	150 ml (¼ pint) beef stock
45 ml (3 tbsp) vegetable oil	10 ml (2 level tsp) ground cumin	salt and freshly ground pepper
5 ml (1 level tsp) ginger	900 g (2 lb) blade of beef	

SERVES 6

Combine the soured cream, garlic, tomato purée and oil. Stir in the ginger, turmeric, coriander, curry powder and cumin.

Trim any sinew from the beef. Pierce the meat all over with a fine skewer. Place in an ovenproof casserole and spoon over the marinade, coating well. Leave for 4–6 hours.

Cover the casserole. Cook in the oven at 170°C (325°F) mark 3 for about 2 hours.

Stir the rice, parsley and stock into the juices surrounding the meat. Season. Cook covered for a further 35 minutes until the rice is tender and most of the juices are absorbed.

Not suitable for freezing.

Ragù Bolognese

In Italy every cook or restaurant claims to prepare the best *ragù*, which can only mean that the variations are endless. Some cooks add chicken livers, others mushrooms, some use minced beef and minced pork or sausage, some add cream at the end, others milk at the beginning and so on. One thing always applies: you should cook the *ragù* over a very low heat and for a long time. This is a good standard recipe, on which you can base your own variations if you wish.

25 g (1 oz) butter
2 slices of unsmoked streaky bacon, finely chopped
1 small onion, skinned and finely chopped
1 small carrot, peeled and finely chopped

45 ml (3 tbsp) vegetable oil
1 small celery stick, finely chopped
1 small garlic clove, skinned and finely chopped
1 bayleaf
25 ml (1½ tbsp) tomato purée

225 g (8 oz) best minced beef
100 ml (4 fl oz) dry white wine
100 ml (4 fl oz) beef stock
salt and freshly ground pepper

SERVES 4

Heat the butter and oil in a saucepan and cook the bacon for 1 minute. Add the onion and, when it begins to soften, the carrot, celery, garlic and bay leaf. Stir and cook for 2 minutes. Add the tomato purée and cook over a low heat for 30 seconds. Put in the minced beef and cook briskly for 3–4 minutes until the meat has lost its raw colour. Add the wine and boil for about 4 minutes until the liquid has almost evaporated. Discard the bayleaf and pour in the stock. Mix well, season and simmer, covered, for about 2 hours, adding a little warm water if the sauce becomes too dry.

Suitable for freezing. Reheat in the usual way.

Chilli con Carne

225 g (8 oz) dried red kidney beans, soaked overnight
2 medium onions, skinned and chopped
700 g (1½ lb) lean minced beef

15 ml (1 tbsp) vegetable oil
1 large garlic clove, skinned and crushed
15 ml (1 level tbsp) salt
freshly ground pepper
793-g (28-oz) can tomatoes

30–45 ml (2–3 level tbsp) chilli seasoning or 2.5 ml (½ level tsp) chilli powder
15 ml (1 level tbsp) flour
30 ml (2 level tbsp) tomato purée

SERVES 6

Drain the beans and place in a saucepan of water. Bring to the boil and boil rapidly for 10 minutes then boil gently for about 45 minutes until tender. In a large saucepan, fry the onion in the oil, add the mince and cook until brown and crumbly. Add the garlic, salt, pepper and chilli seasoning to the mince. Sprinkle on the flour and stir it in. Add the tomato purée and the tomatoes with their juice. Bring to the boil and add the drained beans. Reduce the heat, cover and simmer for 30 minutes, stirring occasionally. Serve with rice.

Note For convenience, a 213 g (7½ oz) can red kidney beans can be used. Drain and add the beans 10 minutes before the cooking time is completed.

Suitable for freezing. Reheat in the usual way.

Rich Beef and Wine Casserole

The initial browning of the meat and onion is most important to the finished result.

1.1 kg (2½ lb) chuck steak in
a piece
45 ml (3 tbsp) vegetable oil
4 medium onions, about
350 g (12 oz) skinned
45 ml (3 tbsp) brandy

1 large garlic clove, skinned
and crushed
200 ml (7 fl oz) red wine
200 ml (7 fl oz) beef stock
salt and freshly ground
pepper

2 bayleaves
10 ml (2 level tsp) cornflour
900 g (2 lb) medium potatoes
225 g (8 oz) button
mushrooms

SERVES 6

Cut the beef into large squares about 5 cm (2 inch) each. Heat the oil in a large, shallow flameproof casserole and brown the pieces of meat a few at a time. Take out of the pan and set aside.

Meanwhile quarter the onions then brown well in the residual oil; remove from the pan and keep on one side. Replace the meat and flame with brandy. Add the garlic with the red wine, stock, bayleaves and seasoning and bring just to the boil. Cover the casserole tightly and cook in the oven at 170°C (325°F) mark 3 for 1 hour.

Meanwhile peel the potatoes and cut into finger sized pieces and keep them under water. Wipe the mushrooms well and quarter if large. After 1 hour take the casserole out of the oven.

Blend the cornflour to a smooth paste with a little water and stir into the casserole. Bring to the boil on top of the cooker, stirring all the time. Stir the drained potatoes, onions and mushrooms into the casserole, replace the lid and return to the oven for a further 1—1¼ hours, or until the meat and vegetables are tender.

Adjust seasoning and scatter over chopped parsley just before serving.

Suitable for freezing. Reheat in the usual way.

Calcutta Curry

550 g (1¼ lb) shin of beef
25 g (1 oz) lard
300 ml (½ pint) water
2 medium onions, skinned
and sliced

1 garlic clove, skinned and
crushed
15 ml (1 level tbsp) hot curry
powder
2.5 ml (½ level tsp) turmeric

2.5 ml (½ level tsp) ground
cumin
150 ml (¼ pint) milk
salt to taste

SERVES 4

Cut the meat into 3-cm (1¼-inch) cubes. Melt half the lard in a heavy saucepan or flameproof casserole and fry the meat cubes quickly to seal. Stir in the water, cover and simmer very gently for about 1½ hours until the beef is tender. Melt the remaining lard in another pan and fry the onion for 5 minutes until golden brown. Stir in the garlic and spices and fry gently, stirring, for a further 4—5 minutes. Blend in the milk, then add to the cooked meat with the salt. Simmer, uncovered, for about 10 minutes or until the juices are reduced slightly. Serve with plain boiled rice and poppadums.

Not suitable for freezing.

Flemish Beef in Beer

1 kg (2¼ lb) chuck steak or thick flank
45 ml (3 tbsp) melted dripping or oil
200 g (7 oz) button onions, skinned

30 ml (2 level tbsp) flour
finely grated rind and juice of 1 orange
150 ml (¼ pint) water
300 ml (½ pint) pale ale
pinch of grated nutmeg

2.5 ml (½ level tsp) dried rosemary
salt and freshly ground pepper

SERVES 6

Cut the meat into 5-cm (2-inch) cubes. Heat the dripping or oil in a flameproof casserole; fry the meat quickly until it is browned on all sides. Remove the meat and cook the whole onions in remaining fat until they are browned. Stir in the flour and return the meat to pan. Add the orange rind and juice, water and ale. Stir well, then add the rosemary and nutmeg. Season well and bring to the boil, stirring all the time.

Cover and cook in the oven at 170°C (325°F) mark 3 for 1½–2 hours.

If wished serve with a potato 'collar'. With a large star nozzle, pipe creamed potato round the edge and brown under a hot grill.

Suitable for freezing. Freeze without the potato 'collar'. Reheat in the usual way and add potato 'collar' if used.

Braised Brisket with Red Wine

15 ml (1 level tbsp) flour
salt and freshly ground pepper
1.1 kg (2¼ lb) piece lean rolled brisket
225 g (8 oz) carrot, peeled and diced

15 ml (1 tbsp) vegetable oil
225 g (8 oz) parsnip, peeled and diced
2 medium onions, skinned and diced
15 ml (1 level tbsp) tomato purée

150 ml (¼ pint) beef stock
60 ml (4 tbsp) red wine
2.5 ml (½ level tsp) dried thyme
bayleaf
10 ml (2 level tsp) cornflour

SERVES 6

Season the flour and roll the brisket joint in it until well coated. Heat the oil in a 2.3-litre (4-pint) flameproof casserole and brown the joint well. Remove the meat and stir the vegetables into the residual fat and sauté for 2 minutes. Add the stock, tomato purée, wine, thyme, bayleaf and seasoning. Bring to the boil. Replace the meat pushing it well down into the vegetables. Cover tightly and cook in the oven at 170°C (325°F) mark 3 for about 2¼ hours or until the meat is tender when pierced with a fine skewer. Remove the meat and carve into slices. Arrange on a serving dish with the vegetables, cover and keep warm. Mix the cornflour to a paste with a little water. Stir into the juices, bring slowly to the boil and cook for 2–3 minutes to thicken. Adjust the seasoning and serve separately.

Not suitable for freezing.

Chiddingly Hot Pot

This recipe was said to have been created by one Edward Shoosmith of Strete Chiddingly, in 1917. Best undercut of sirloin was used at that time, but here lean stewing steak is used as a cheaper substitute.

450 g (1 lb) onions, skinned and chopped

1 head celery, wiped and chopped

100 g (4 oz) black olives, stoned and roughly chopped

900 g (2 lb) stewing steak, cubed

90 ml (6 tbsp) red wine vinegar

8 whole allspice

8 cloves

4 blades mace

salt and freshly ground pepper

900 g (2 lb) potatoes, peeled and thinly sliced

600 ml (1 pint) beef stock

SERVES 6–8

In a really large ovenproof casserole, layer onions, celery, olives, stewing beef (each time sprinkling meat with vinegar and seasonings) and potatoes. Finish with a layer of potatoes, pour over the stock, cover and cook in the oven at 170°C (325°F) mark 3 for about 2½ hours until the meat is tender.

Suitable for freezing. Reheat in the usual way.

Braised Beef with Soured Cream

575 g (1¼ lb) boned top rib beef

45 ml (3 tbsp) vegetable oil

1 medium onion, skinned and sliced

30 ml (2 level tbsp) flour

300 ml (½ pint) beef stock

salt and freshly ground pepper

1 small green pepper, halved, seeded and sliced

chopped parsley, to garnish

175 g (6 oz) button mushrooms, wiped and sliced

142 ml (5 fl oz) soured cream, stirred

SERVES 4

Slice the meat into strips about 5 cm (2 inch) long by 1 cm (½ inch) wide. Brown them in hot oil in a small flameproof casserole and then remove with a draining spoon. Add the onion and lightly brown. Stir in the flour and cook for 1 minute. Remove from the heat and mix in the stock and seasoning and bring to the boil, stirring. Replace the meat, cover tightly and cook in the oven at 170°C (325°F) mark 3 for about 1¾ hours. Stir in the pepper and mushrooms, cover and return to oven for 15 minutes. Stir the soured cream through. Adjust the seasoning. Sprinkle with chopped parsley.

Suitable for freezing. Freeze without soured cream and reheat in the usual way, and add soured cream.

Beef in Port Wine

For a milder taste, use shallots instead of onion.

900 g (2 lb) chuck steak
150 ml (¼ pint) port
1 garlic clove, skinned
    and crushed
salt and freshly ground
    pepper

45 ml (3 tbsp) vegetable oil
25 g (1 oz) butter or
    margarine
350 g (12 oz) very small
    onions, skinned
150 ml (¼ pint) beef stock

225 g (½ lb) lambs' kidneys
225 g (½ lb) small button
    mushrooms
15 ml (1 level tbsp) cornflour

SERVES 4–6

Cut chuck steak into strips about 5 × 1 cm (2 × ½ inch). Mix the port, crushed garlic and seasonings together and pour over the meat. Cover and refrigerate overnight. Drain off the marinade and reserve. Brown the meat, a few pieces at a time, in the hot oil and butter in a flameproof casserole. Take the meat out of the pan and lightly brown the onions. Pour in the stock, reserved marinade and seasoning and bring to the boil. Replace the meat, cover and cook in the oven at 170°C (325°F) mark 3 for 1½ hours. Meanwhile skin, halve and core the kidneys and cut the flesh into small pieces. Wipe the button mushrooms – cut them in half if they are large. Stir the kidneys and mushrooms into the casserole, cover and return to the oven for a further 30 minutes, or until the meat is tender. Mix the cornflour to a smooth paste with a little water. Stir into the casserole then bring slowly to the boil, stirring gently all the time. Cook for 2–3 minutes and then adjust seasoning.

Suitable for freezing. Freeze without thickening. Reheat in the usual way and add thickening.

Carbonade of Beef

900 g (2 lb) stewing steak,
    cut into 1-cm (½-inch)
    cubes
salt and freshly ground
    pepper
50 g (2 oz) beef dripping or
    butter

75 g (3 oz) lean bacon,
    rinded and chopped
60 ml (4 level tbsp) plain
    flour
300 ml (½ pint) beer
300 ml (½ pint) beef stock or
    water

30–45 ml (2–3 tbsp) vinegar
450 g (1 lb) onions, skinned
    and chopped
1 garlic clove, skinned and
    chopped
bouquet garni

SERVES 4

Season the meat and fry in the fat for about 5 minutes until brown. Add the bacon and continue cooking for a few minutes. Remove the meat and bacon from the pan, stir in the flour and brown lightly. Gradually add the beer, stock and vinegar, stirring continuously until the mixture thickens. Fill a casserole with layers of meat, bacon, onion and garlic. Pour the sauce over and add the bouquet garni. Cover and cook in the oven at 150°C (300°F) mark 2 for 3½–4 hours. Add a little more beer while cooking, if necessary. Just before serving, remove the bouquet garni. Serve with plain boiled potatoes.

Suitable for freezing. Reheat in the usual way.

Boeuf Bourguignonne

100 g (4 oz) bacon, in a piece
50 g (2 oz) butter
30 ml (2 tbsp) vegetable oil
900 g (2 lb) braising steak or
   topside, cubed
45 ml (3 level tbsp) flour

1 garlic clove, skinned and
   crushed
salt and freshly ground
   pepper
bouquet garni
150 ml (¼ pint) beef stock

300 ml (½ pint) red wine,
   preferably burgundy
12 small onions, skinned
6 oz button mushrooms,
   wiped
chopped parsley to garnish

SERVES 4

Dice the bacon. Melt half the butter and oil in a large flameproof casserole. Quickly brown the bacon and drain. Reheat the fat and brown the meat in small amounts. Return the bacon to the casserole with the garlic. Sprinkle the flour over and stir in well. Add salt and pepper, the bouquet garni, stock and wine. Bring to the boil, stirring all the time. Cover and cook in the oven at 170°C (325°F) mark 3 for about 1½ hours.

Meanwhile heat remaining butter and oil together. Sauté the whole onions until they are glazed and golden brown. Remove from the pan and sauté the mushrooms. Remove the mushrooms and add them with the onions to the casserole and cook for a further 30 minutes. Remove the bouquet garni. Skim off the surface fat. Serve garnished with chopped parsley.

Suitable for freezing. Reheat in the usual way.

Chunky Beef with Celery

50 g (2 oz) red kidney beans,
   soaked overnight
four 125 g (4 oz) chunky
   pieces top rib beef
25 g (1 oz) lard or dripping

225 g (8 oz) trimmed celery
1 medium onion, skinned
   and sliced
400 ml (¾ pint) herb stock

30 ml (2 tbsp) sherry
salt and freshly ground
   pepper
30 ml (2 level tbsp) cornflour

SERVES 4

Drain the beans and place in a saucepan of water. Bring to the boil and boil rapidly for 10 minutes, then drain again.

Brown the pieces of beef in the hot fat in a flameproof casserole. Remove from the fat.

Wash the celery and slice it into 5-cm (2-inch) lengths. Add the celery and onion to the casserole and lightly brown. Mix in the beans. Sit the meat on top of the vegetables. Pour the stock and sherry over and season well. Bring to the boil. Cover and bake in the oven at 170°C (325°F) mark 4 for about 2 hours.

Strain off the liquid and thicken with the cornflour mixed to a smooth paste with a little water. Bubble for a few minutes. Adjust seasoning. Serve the stew in a shallow dish with some of the sauce spooned over. Serve the rest separately.

Suitable for freezing. Freeze without thickening. Reheat in the usual way and thicken with the cornflour paste.

Lamb

Lamb casseroles are not confined to the traditional English Lancashire Hot Pot or the classic Irish Stew – in fact, lamb recipes from all over the world seem to have been creeping more and more into good cooks' repertoires over the last few years. Lamb absorbs spices especially well and included here are dishes combining the aromatic flavours of cumin, coriander, turmeric and ginger with the delicate succulence of the meat. Mint and rosemary, of course, are classic accompaniments to lamb, and many fruits, such as oranges, lemons or apricots, give a delicious tang to its mellow flavour.

Good economical cuts for casseroling are middle or scrag end, shoulder or shank end, or breast, which though inclined to be fatty is tender and well-flavoured, and the fat can always be absorbed by potatoes, as in Irish Stew, or as is often better, by cooling the casserole and removing the solidified fat before reheating.

Lamb Casserole with Orange and Rosemary Dumplings

25 g (1 oz) dripping
225 g (8 oz) button onions, skinned
225 g (8 oz) carrots, peeled and thinly sliced
8 best end of neck lamb chops
25 g (1 oz) flour
400 ml (¾ pint) chicken stock

grated rind and juice of 1 orange
15 ml (1 tbsp) Worcestershire sauce
30 ml (2 level tbsp) tomato purée
salt and freshly ground pepper

For the dumplings
175 g (6 oz) self-raising flour
75 g (3 oz) shredded suet
salt and freshly ground pepper
5 ml (1 level tsp) dried rosemary
grated rind and juice of 1 orange

SERVES 4

Melt the dripping in a large frying pan and cook the onions and carrots for about 5 minutes until golden brown. Remove from the pan and put into a large casserole. Fry the lamb chops for 5 minutes on each side and add to the casserole.

Stir the flour into the remaining fat and gradually add the stock and the orange rind and juice. Bring to the boil, stirring continuously. Add the remaining ingredients and pour over the chops. Cover and cook in the oven at 170°C (325°F) mark 3 for 1 hour.

Meanwhile, make up the dumplings. Mix all the ingredients together and add enough water to make a soft dough. Roll into 16 small balls. Put the dumplings into the casserole, cover and cook in the oven at 190°C (375°F) mark 5 for a further 20 minutes, until the dumplings are well risen.

Serve with fresh green vegetables or salad.

Suitable for freezing. Freeze without dumplings. Reheat in the usual way and add dumplings and finish as above.

Beef in Brandy and Mustard (see page 23)

Minted Lamb Casserole

4 lamb chump chops or
700 g (1½ lb) middle neck,
chopped
freshly ground pepper
25 g (1 oz) lard
1 medium onion, skinned
and chopped

397-g (14-oz) can peeled
tomatoes
pinch of garlic salt
2.5 ml (½ level tsp) salt
5 ml (1 level tsp) dried mint
or 15 ml (1 level tbsp)
chopped fresh mint

5 ml (1 level tsp) sugar
1 bayleaf
50 g (2 oz) Cheddar cheese,
grated
50 g (2 oz) fresh
breadcrumbs

SERVES 4

Trim excess fat from the chops and remove bone. Sprinkle both sides of the meat with
pepper. Heat the lard in a pan and brown the chops on both sides. Drain on kitchen
paper to remove most of the fat. Fry the chopped onion in the remaining fat in pan for
about 3 minutes. Remove using a draining spoon and place in an ovenproof casserole
with the chops. Mix the tomatoes with their juices, seasonings, sugar and herbs. Pour
over the meat. Cover and cook in the oven at 170°C (325°F) mark 3 for 1 hour.
Remove the bayleaf. Remove the lid and sprinkle over the cheese and breadcrumbs
mixed together. Bake, uncovered, for a further 30 minutes until golden.

*Suitable for freezing. Freeze without the cheese and breadcrumbs. Reheat in the usual way and add
topping.*

Lamb with Almonds

If you use lamb shoulder instead of leg, buy one weighing about 2.5 kg (5½ lb) to
allow for wastage when trimming. You need about 1.1 kg (2½ lb) lean meat.

2 kg (4½ lb) leg of lamb on
bone
60 ml (4 tbsp) vegetable oil
225 g (8 oz) onion, skinned
and finely chopped
5 ml (1 level tsp) paprika

15 ml (1 level tbsp) ground
ginger
75 g (3 oz) ground almonds
75 ml (3 fl oz) chicken stock
300 ml (½ pint) single cream

1 garlic clove, skinned and
crushed
salt and freshly ground pepper
25 g (1 oz) fresh root ginger
snipped parsley to garnish

SERVES 6

Remove the meat from the bone and cut into 2.5-cm (1-inch) pieces discarding skin and
fat. Heat the oil in a medium-size flameproof casserole and brown the meat a little at
a time. Remove from the pan using draining spoons. Add the onion to the residual oil
and sprinkle over the ground ginger and ground paprika. Cook gently for 1 minute
stirring. Mix in the ground almonds, stock, cream, garlic and seasoning and bring to
the boil. Replace the meat, stir well, cover tightly and cook in the oven at 170°C
(325°F) mark 3 for 1¼ hours.

Peel the root ginger then chop finely; stir into the lamb dish, re-cover and return to
the oven for a further 20 minutes or until the meat is quite tender. Skim well, adjust
seasoning and spoon into a serving dish. Garnish with snipped parsley.

Not suitable for freezing.

Lancashire Hot Pot (see page 41)

Irish Stew

8 middle neck chops	2 large onions, skinned and	salt and freshly ground
900 g (2 lb) potatoes, peeled	sliced	pepper
and sliced	chopped parsley to garnish	

SERVES 4

Trim some of the fat from the chops. Place alternate layers of vegetables and meat in a saucepan, seasoning with salt and pepper and finishing with a layer of potatoes. Add sufficient water to half cover. Cover with a lid and simmer very slowly for 3 hours. Serve sprinkled with chopped parsley.

Alternatively, cook the stew in a casserole in the oven at 190°C (375°F) mark 5 for 2½–3 hours.

If you use scrag end of neck for Irish stew it makes an economical dish.

Not suitable for freezing.

Lamb Noisettes with Pepper and Courgettes

Illustrated in colour on the jacket

12 noisettes of lamb	1 garlic clove, skinned and	225 g (8 oz) courgettes,
flour for coating	finely chopped	trimmed and sliced
25 g (1 oz) butter	225 g (8 oz) button	30 ml (2 tbsp) tomato purée
60 ml (4 tbsp) vegetable oil	mushrooms, wiped	2 bayleaves
2 large onions, skinned	1 small red pepper, seeded	salt and freshly ground
and sliced	and sliced	pepper
300 ml (½ pint) red wine	150 ml (¼ pint) chicken stock	

SERVES 6

Lightly coat the lamb with flour. Heat the butter and oil in a large flameproof casserole. Add the noisettes, a few at a time, and brown quickly on both sides. Remove from the casserole. Add the onion and garlic and fry for about 5 minutes until golden. Add the mushrooms, pepper and courgettes and fry for a further 2–3 minutes. Stir in the red wine, stock, tomato purée and bayleaves. Season well with salt and pepper. Replace the noisettes, bring to the boil then cover and simmer gently for about 40 minutes until tender. Turn the meat once during the cooking time. Remove the string from the noisettes before serving.

Suitable for freezing. Reheat in the usual way.

Lamb with Orange Sauce

2 large breasts of lean lamb,
    boned
75 g (3 oz) fresh
    breadcrumbs
2 oranges
2.5 ml (½ level tsp) dried mint

1 egg, beaten
salt and freshly ground
    pepper
4 medium onions, skinned
300 ml (½ pint) chicken stock
10 ml (2 level tsp) cornflour

5 ml (1 level tsp) demerara
    sugar
5 ml (1 tsp) Worcestershire
    sauce

SERVES 4

Trim excess fat from the lamb. Combine breadcrumbs, grated rind from 1 orange (prepare the segments, free of white pith for garnish), mint, egg and seasoning. Spread over the meat, roll up and tie with string. Place the lamb in an ovenproof casserole with the onions (halved crosswise, cut-side up). Season with salt and pepper. Add 60 ml (4 tbsp) stock. Cover the casserole and cook in the oven at 180°C (350°F) mark 4 for about 50 minutes, uncover for the last 20 minutes to brown. Meanwhile, in a small pan, blend a little of the remaining stock with the cornflour, then add the rest with the sugar, Worcestershire sauce and the grated rind and juice from second orange. Bring to the boil, stirring and cook for 1–2 minutes. Season.

Serve the lamb in thick slices with the orange sauce and reserved segments. Accompany with noodles.

Not suitable for freezing.

Oriental Lamb

900 g (2 lb) lamb shoulder,
    boned
15 ml (1 tbsp) vegetable oil
450 g (1 lb) white cabbage,
    trimmed and shredded
175 g (6 oz) carrot, peeled
    and finely sliced
1 small green pepper, seeded
    and chopped

1 medium onion, skinned
    and thinly sliced
30 ml (2 tbsp) soy sauce
15 ml (1 tbsp)
    Worcestershire sauce
30 ml (2 tbsp) wine vinegar
15 ml (1 level tbsp) brown
    sugar
600 ml (1 pint) stock

5 ml (1 level tsp) dried
    rosemary
salt and freshly ground
    pepper
1 cap canned pimiento,
    thinly sliced
25 g (1 oz) noodles

SERVES 4

Trim the lamb of excess fat and cut into 2.5-cm (1-inch) cubes. Heat the oil in a flameproof casserole, add the lamb and brown, turning occasionally. Stir in the cabbage, carrot, pepper and onion and cook gently for 5 minutes. Meanwhile mix soy sauce, Worcestershire sauce, vinegar, sugar and stock together, pour over lamb mixture, sprinkle in rosemary and season well. Cover and simmer on top of cooker, stirring occasionally, for about 50 minutes. Add the pimiento and noodles to the lamb stirring well to mix and continue to bubble gently for a further 15 minutes until noodles are cooked *al dente.*

Suitable for freezing. Freeze without pimiento and noodles. Reheat in the usual way and add pimiento and noodles.

Lamb in Horseradish Sauce

This unusual Italian recipe is from Friuli, where there is a strong Yugoslav influence, which accounts for the use of horseradish in this dish.

75 g (3 oz) butter
30 ml (2 tbsp) vegetable oil
1 onion, skinned and sliced
2.5 ml (½ level tsp) dried
   thyme
3 bayleaves
90 ml (6 tbsp) wine vinegar

175 ml (6 fl oz) beef stock
salt and freshly ground black
   pepper
1.75 kg (3½ lb) shoulder of
   lamb, boned and cut into
   2.5-cm (1-inch) cubes, with
   fat and gristle removed

45 ml (3 level tbsp)
   horseradish sauce (not
   creamed)
60 ml (4 tbsp) chopped fresh
   parsley

SERVES 4

Put 25 g (1 oz) of the butter, the oil, onion, thyme, bayleaves, vinegar, stock and salt and pepper into a flameproof casserole and bring slowly to the boil. Add the meat and simmer, covered, over a moderate heat for about 1½ hours, until meat is tender. If the meat becomes too dry, add a few tablespoons of warm water during the cooking. When the meat is ready, there should be hardly any liquid in the pan. If there is too much liquid, turn up the heat and reduce in an uncovered pan.

Melt the remaining butter in a small saucepan, then add the horseradish and the parsley and cook, stirring constantly, for 30 seconds. Pour the horseradish sauce over the lamb, amalgamate it with the cooking liquid and turn the meat over once or twice. Taste and adjust the seasonings.

Not suitable for freezing.

Eastern Casserole of Lamb

1.4 kg (3 lb) lean boned lamb
   or mutton
450 g (1 lb) tomatoes,
   skinned
45 ml (3 tbsp) vegetable oil
350 g (12 oz) onion, skinned
   and sliced
1.25 ml (¼ level tsp) turmeric

30 ml (2 level tbsp) ground
   coriander
10 ml (2 level tsp) ground
   cumin
5 ml (1 level tsp) ground
   ginger
1.25 ml (¼ level tsp) cayenne
   pepper

30 ml (2 level tbsp) flour
15 ml (1 level tbsp) tomato
   purée
450 ml (¾ pint) chicken stock
75 g (3 oz) sultanas
salt and freshly ground
   pepper

SERVES 8

Cut the meat into largish chunks. Quarter the tomatoes; push the seeds through a sieve and keep the juice. Heat the oil in a large flameproof casserole. Brown the meat well, a few pieces at a time, then remove from the casserole. Brown the onions in the residual fat. Add the coriander, cumin, ginger, turmeric and cayenne and cook for 2 minutes, then add the flour and cook for 2 minutes. Add remaining ingredients and season well. Replace the meat, cover the casserole and cook in the oven at 170°C (325°F) mark 3 for about 1¾ hours for lamb, 2½ hours for mutton. Serve with rice.

Suitable for freezing. Reheat in the usual way.

Lamb Cutlets in Whisky

Slices of lamb cut from the top end of a small leg can be treated in a similar way.

12 lamb cutlets
450 g (1 lb) carrots, peeled
450 g (1 lb) parsnips, peeled
45 ml (3 tbsp) vegetable oil
120 ml (8 tbsp) whisky

1 medium onion, skinned
  and sliced
150 ml (¼ pint) chicken stock
1 large garlic clove, skinned
  and crushed

salt and freshly ground
  pepper
snipped parsley to garnish

SERVES 6

Trim the cutlets leaving a thin covering of fat. Cut the carrots into fat 'matchsticks' and the parsnips into 0.5-cm (¼-inch) slices. Heat the oil in a medium sized frying pan and brown the cutlets well on both sides, a few at a time. Remove from the pan.

Add the vegetables to the pan and brown lightly. Use a draining spoon to remove them and transfer to a large shallow ovenproof dish. Add whisky to the pan and ignite. Pour in the stock and bring to the boil. Add the garlic, season well. Place the cutlets on the vegetables in a single layer. Pour over the stock, cover tightly with a lid or foil. Cook in the oven at 170°C (325°F) mark 3 for about 1¼ hours or until the cutlets and vegetables are just tender. Scatter generously with snipped parsley before serving.

Suitable for freezing. Reheat in the usual way.

Lamb Mogador

The excellent mellowed flavour of this dish comes from just the right balance of spices; leave any of them out and it's simply not the same.

1.8-kg (4-lb) shoulder of
  lamb to give 1.1 kg (2½ lb)
  meat
1 onion, skinned
1 garlic clove, skinned and
  crushed
2 green chillies
25 g (1 oz) desiccated coconut

30 ml (2 level tbsp) ground
  coriander
5 ml (1 level tsp) turmeric
45 ml (3 tbsp) natural yogurt
45 ml (3 tbsp) vegetable oil
5 ml (1 level tsp) ground
  ginger
400 ml (¾ pint) chicken stock

15 ml (1 level tbsp) sesame
  seeds
salt and freshly ground
  pepper
50 g (2 oz) cashew nuts,
  chopped

SERVES 6

Cut the flesh off the bone, discarding most of the fat and divide it into fork-size pieces. Finely chop the onion and put in the bowl with garlic. Halve the chillies, remove seeds and chop finely (wear rubber gloves in case the fresh chillies give you sore fingers). Add them to the onion with the coconut, coriander, turmeric and yogurt. Stir well. Heat the oil in large shallow saucepan or sauté pan. Add meat, sprinkle with ginger and lightly brown it. Stir in the onion mixture and cook gently for 10 minutes, stirring frequently. Add the sesame seeds with the stock and seasoning; bring to the boil, reduce heat and *simmer* covered for 30 minutes. Uncover and cook a further ¾ hour, or until tender. Adjust the seasoning. To serve, scatter with cashews.

Not suitable for freezing.

Lamb with Red Wine

A little wine makes a lot of difference to a dish. For a better flavour, reduce 200–300 ml ($\frac{1}{3}$–$\frac{1}{2}$ pint) *vin ordinaire* to 150 ml ($\frac{1}{4}$ pint) by fast bubbling.

1.6 kg (3½ lb) leg of lamb	150 ml (¼ pint) red wine	15 ml (1 level tbsp) plain
45 ml (3 tbsp) coarsely	salt and freshly ground	flour
chopped fresh mint	pepper	dash of gravy browning
2 medium onions, skinned	45 ml (3 tbsp) vegetable oil	
and thickly sliced	150 ml (¼ pint) chicken stock	

SERVES 6

Cut all the meat away from the bone in largish pieces, discard skin and fat. Slice the meat into narrow finger-size pieces.

In a medium sized bowl combine meat, onion and mint. Pour over the red wine, season well and stir together. Cover tightly with cling film and leave to marinate in the refrigerator for at least 8 hours. Strain off the marinade and reserve.

Heat the oil in a flameproof casserole and brown the meat and onions well, half at a time. Replace the meat and onions in the casserole and stir in the flour followed by the reserved marinade and stock. Bring to the boil, adjust the seasoning. Cover the casserole and cook in the oven at 170°C (325°F) mark 3 for 1¼–1½ hours, or until the meat is quite tender. Use a draining spoon to lift the meat into a shallow serving dish. Boil the cooking liquor to reduce slightly, adjust the seasoning and add gravy browning if necessary. Spoon the juices over the meat. Snip some extra mint over the casserole for serving. Serve with courgettes and new potatoes in their jackets.

Suitable for freezing. Reheat in the usual way.

Blanquette d'Agneau

700 g (1½ lb) boneless lean	2 sticks of celery, trimmed	25 g (1 oz) butter,
shoulder of lamb, diced	and sliced	softened
100 g (4 oz) carrots, peeled	5 ml (1 level tsp) dried thyme	45 ml (3 level tbsp) flour
and sliced	salt and freshly ground	1 egg yolk
100 g (4 oz) onions, skinned	pepper	30 ml (2 tbsp) cream or milk
and sliced	300 ml (½ pint) chicken stock	chopped parsley to garnish
small bayleaf	or water	

SERVES 4

Put the meat, carrots, onions, celery, flavourings and seasonings in a large pan. Cover with stock or water, put the lid on and simmer for 1½ hours. Blend together the softened butter and flour; when they are thoroughly mixed, add to the stew in small knobs and stir until thickened; simmer for 10 minutes, adding more liquid if necessary. Blend together the egg yolk and cream, add to the stew and reheat without boiling. Garnish with parsley before serving.

Suitable for freezing. Freeze without butter, flour, egg and cream. Reheat in the usual way and thicken as above.

Oriental Lamb Sauté

1.4 kg (3 lb) shoulder of
　lamb
30 ml (2 tbsp) vegetable oil
25 g (1 oz) butter
450 g (1 lb) small new
　potatoes, scraped

225 g ($\frac{1}{2}$ lb) small onions,
　skinned
5 ml (1 level tsp) ground
　ginger
15 ml (1 level tbsp) flour
300 ml ($\frac{1}{2}$ pint) beef stock

15 ml (1 tbsp)
　Worcestershire sauce
30 ml (2 tbsp) soy sauce
salt and freshly ground
　pepper
2 caps canned pimiento

SERVES 4

Slice all the meat off the bone, discarding excess fat, and cut it into 2.5-cm (1-inch)
pieces about 0.5 cm ($\frac{1}{4}$ inch) thick. Heat the oil and butter in a large sauté pan and
brown the meat a few pieces at a time. Remove the meat from the pan. Lightly brown
the potatoes and onions in the residual oil and replace the meat. Sprinkle the flour
and ginger into the pan, stir well and cook gently for 2 minutes. Add the stock,
Worcestershire sauce, soy sauce and seasoning, bring to the boil, cover and simmer for
1$\frac{1}{4}$ hours. Dice the pimiento, add to the sauté and stir over a low heat to bring it to
serving temperature.

Not suitable for freezing.

Lamb and Cider Hot-Pot

1.8 kg (4 lb) lamb shoulder,
　boned
50 g (2 oz) flour
90 ml (6 tbsp) vegetable oil
90 g (3$\frac{1}{2}$ oz) butter
600 ml (1 pint) chicken stock

225 g ($\frac{1}{2}$ lb) onion, skinned
　and sliced
350 g ($\frac{3}{4}$ lb) celery, wiped and
　chopped
450 g (1 lb) cooking apples,
　peeled, cored and sliced

327-ml (11$\frac{1}{2}$-fl oz) can cider
salt and freshly ground
　pepper
450 g (1 lb) potatoes, thinly
　sliced
parsley sprigs to garnish

SERVES 8

Cut the meat into 5-cm (2-inch) pieces, discarding any fat. Toss in flour and brown
quickly in oil mixed with 50 g (2 oz) butter in a frying pan. Drain and put in a 2.8-litre
(5-pint) capacity pie or ovenproof dish, sprinkling in any excess flour. Add onions,
celery and apples to the frying pan and brown lightly; spoon on top of the meat. Pour
the stock and cider with plenty of seasoning over meat and vegetables. Top with a
layer of potatoes and dot with remaining butter. Stand the dish on a baking sheet and
bake in the oven at 180°C (350°F) mark 4 about 1$\frac{1}{2}$ hours, or until meat is tender and
potatoes crisp; serve garnished with parsley.

Suitable for freezing. Reheat in the usual way.

Navarin of Lamb

This is a traditional dish of French origin.

1 kg (2¼ lb) best end of neck, divided into cutlets
30 ml (2 tbsp) vegetable oil
5 ml (1 level tsp) sugar
15 ml (1 level tbsp) flour
900 ml (1½ pint) chicken stock or water
30 ml (2 tbsp) tomato purée
salt and freshly ground pepper
bouquet garni
4 onions, skinned and quartered
4 carrots, peeled and sliced
1–2 turnips, peeled and quartered
8 small, even sized potatoes, peeled
chopped parsley to garnish

SERVES 4

Fry the cutlets lightly on all sides in the oil. If there is too much fat at this stage, pour off a little to leave 15–30 ml (1–2 tbsp). Stir in the sugar and heat until it browns slightly, then add the flour, stirring until this also cooks and browns. Remove from the heat, stir in the stock gradually, then bring to the boil and add the tomato purée, seasoning and bouquet garni. Cover, reduce the heat and simmer for about 1 hour. Remove the bouquet garni, add the onions, carrots and turnips and continue cooking for another 30 minutes. Finally, add the potatoes and continue cooking for about 20 minutes, until tender.

Serve the meat on a heated serving dish, surrounded by the vegetables and garnished with the parsley.

Note A 112-g (4-oz) packet of frozen peas can also be added to the mixture about 10 minutes before it is served.

Suitable for freezing. Freeze without potatoes. Reheat in the usual way and add potatoes, and peas if used.

Lamb and Leek Boulangère

700 g (1½ lb) potatoes, peeled and thinly sliced
450 g (1 lb) leeks, sliced, washed and drained
225 g (8 oz) onions, skinned and sliced
700 g (1½ lb) boned shoulder of lamb, coarsely minced
10 ml (2 level tsp) dried rosemary
salt and freshly ground pepper
2 beef stock cubes
30 ml (2 level tbsp) cornflour
150 ml (¼ pint) water
75 g (3 oz) Cheddar cheese, grated

SERVES 6

Line the base of a 2-litre (3½-pint) ovenproof dish with half the potato slices. Place alternate layers of leeks, onions and minced lamb in the dish, sprinkling rosemary, salt and pepper between the layers, and top with the remaining potato slices. Blend the stock cubes and cornflour with the water and pour over. Cover with a lid. Bake in the oven at 200°C (400°F) mark 6 for about 1 hour, or until the potatoes are tender. Uncover and sprinkle with the cheese, and return to the oven for a further 20 minutes until golden.

Not suitable for freezing.

Peppered Lamb Stew

25 g (1 oz) dripping
700 g (1½ lb) middle neck of
  lamb
175 g (6 oz) onions, skinned
  and sliced
30 ml (2 level tbsp) flour

225 g (8 oz) carrots, peeled
  and sliced
225 g (8 oz) turnips, peeled
  and sliced
500 ml (1 pint) water or
  chicken stock

30 ml (2 tbsp)
  Worcestershire sauce
salt and freshly ground
  pepper

SERVES 4

Heat the dripping in a flameproof casserole or saucepan and fry the meat to brown on all sides. Drain the meat and keep on one side. Add the prepared vegetables to the casserole or pan and cook gently for 5 minutes. Add the flour and cook, stirring, until pale golden. Add the liquid and bring to the boil, stirring. Return the meat with Worcestershire sauce and seasoning. Cover and simmer for 1½ hours, or until meat is tender. If you like, add dumplings – (see page 121) – for the last 20 minutes of cooking time (adding extra stock), or serve with boiled pasta or potatoes.

Suitable for freezing. Reheat in the usual way.

Lancashire Hot Pot

One of the best known of Lancashire dishes, the hot pot takes its name from the tall earthenware dish in which it traditionally was cooked. The long boned chops from the Pennine sheep could be stood vertically around the pot and the centre filled with vegetables, kidneys, mushrooms and, in the days when they were cheap, oysters. A thatch of sliced potatoes completed the dish. Pickled red cabbage was eaten with it, but ordinary red cabbage tastes just as good.

900 g (2 lb) middle neck of
  lamb, divided into eight
  cutlets
175 g (6 oz) lambs' kidneys
450 g (1 lb) trimmed leeks

40 g (1½ oz) lard or dripping
225 g (½ lb) carrots, peeled
  and thickly sliced
900 g (2 lb) potatoes, peeled
  and thinly sliced

5 ml (1 level tsp) dried thyme
salt and freshly ground
  pepper
600 ml (1 pint) beef stock

SERVES 4 ———————————————————— *Illustrated in colour opposite page 33*

Trim any excess fat off the lamb; skin, halve and core the kidneys and divide each half into three or four pieces. Slice the leeks into 1-cm (½-inch) thick pieces, discarding the roots, wash and drain well. Heat the lard in a frying pan and brown the lamb, a few pieces at a time. Lightly brown the kidneys. In a 3.4-litre (6-pint) ovenproof casserole layer up the meats, leeks, carrots and three-quarters of the potatoes, sprinkling herbs and seasoning between the layers. Pour in the stock and top with a neat layer of overlapping potato slices. Brush with the residual lard from the frying pan.

Cover the casserole and cook in the oven at 170°C (325°F) mark 3 for 2 hours. Uncover, increase the temperature to 220°C (425°F) mark 7 and continue cooking for about 30 minutes until the top layer of potatoes are golden brown and crisp.

Suitable for freezing. Reheat in the oven at 220°C (425°F) mark 7, loosely covered for about 1¼ hours.

Lamb and Lemon Casserole

450 g (1 lb) minced lamb
75 g (3 oz) fresh
  breadcrumbs
1 lemon
45 ml (3 level tbsp)
  horseradish sauce
7.5 ml (1½ level tsp) ground
  paprika

salt and freshly ground
  pepper
1 egg, size 2, beaten
45 ml (3 level tbsp) plain
  flour
45 ml (3 tbsp) vegetable oil
175 g (6 oz) onions, skinned
  and sliced

1 garlic clove, skinned and
  crushed
185-g (6½-oz) can tomatoes
300 ml (½ pint) chicken
  stock
chopped parsley to garnish

SERVES 4

Combine the lamb with the breadcrumbs, finely grated lemon rind, 15 ml (1 tbsp) lemon juice, horseradish, seasoning and egg. Stir well to blend. Shape into 16 small balls. Toss in flour and brown well in the hot oil in a shallow flameproof casserole. Remove from the oil. Brown the onion in the oil. Stir in any remaining flour with the garlic, tomatoes with juice, stock, 15 ml (1 tbsp) lemon juice and seasoning. Bring to the boil.

Replace the meat balls, cover lightly and cook in the oven at 180°C (350°F) mark 4 for about 40 minutes.

Adjust the seasoning, and garnish with chopped parsley.

Suitable for freezing. Reheat in the usual way.

Lamb in Tomato Sauce

1.4 kg (3 lb) shoulder of lamb,
  boned
700 g (1½ lb) tomatoes,
  skinned
chicken stock
30 ml (2 tbsp) vegetable oil
20 ml (4 level tsp) flour

1 medium onion, skinned
  and sliced
30 ml (2 level tbsp) tomato
  purée
2.5 ml (½ level tsp) dried
  rosemary
parsley or chive butter

60 ml (4 tbsp) red wine
salt and freshly ground
  pepper
8 slices of French bread

SERVES 4

Cut the meat into chunks, discard bone and excess fat. Quarter the tomatoes and push out seeds into a sieve over a jug to collect juices. Make up to 300 ml (½ pint) with stock. Heat the oil in a flameproof casserole and brown the lamb pieces. Remove from the casserole and sauté the onion in residual fat. Stir in the flour and gradually add the measured stock, tomatoes, tomato purée, rosemary and wine. Bring to the boil stirring, replace the meat and season. Cover the casserole and cook in the oven at 170°C (325°F) mark 3 for about 1¼ hours. Spread the herb butter on the French bread. Uncover the casserole, place the bread butter side up on top. Cook for a further 1 hour.

Suitable for freezing. Reheat in the usual way.

Casseroled Lamb with Aubergine

700 g (1½ lb) aubergines
salt and freshly ground
   pepper
1.8–2 kg (4–4½ lb) leg lamb
50 g (2 oz) lard
400 ml (¾ pint) chicken stock

60 ml (4 level tbsp) plain
   flour
90 ml (6 tbsp) medium
   sherry
700 g (1½ lb) tomatoes,
   skinned

5 ml (1 level tsp) dried
   marjoram or 30 ml
   (2 tbsp) fresh chopped
45 ml (3 tbsp) vegetable oil
snipped parsley, to garnish

SERVES 8

Cut the aubergines into 5-mm (¼-inch) slices. Sprinkle with salt and leave for 30 minutes. Rinse under cold water and dry with absorbent kitchen paper.

Meanwhile, cut the lamb off the bone then slice into thin strips. Brown well, a few at a time in the hot lard. Drain from the fat and place in a shallow ovenproof dish. Stir the flour into the pan juices, add stock, sherry and marjoram. Season, bring to the boil and pour over the lamb.

Top with the sliced tomatoes and finally the sliced aubergines. Brush with oil. Cover and bake in the oven at 180°C (350°F) mark 4 for 1½ hours. Uncover; brush the aubergines with the cooking juices and bake at 230°C (450°F) mark 8 for about 20 minutes or until golden. Sprinkle with parsley.

Not suitable for freezing.

Sweet and Sour Lamb with Pasta

4 large breasts of lamb,
   boned and skinned
30 ml (2 tbsp) vegetable oil
225 g (8 oz) onion, skinned
   and sliced
10 ml (2 level tsp) ground
   ginger
300 ml (½ pint) chicken stock

45 ml (3 level tbsp) plain
   flour
300 ml (½ pint) dry cider
30 ml (2 tbsp) soy sauce
15 ml (1 tbsp)
   Worcestershire sauce
45 ml (3 tbsp) thin honey
45 ml (3 tbsp) wine vinegar

340-g (12-oz) can pineapple
   cubes
salt and freshly ground
   pepper
125 g (4 oz) small pasta
   shells
parsley sprigs, to garnish

SERVES 8

Cut up the lamb into 5-cm (2-inch) fingers discarding excess fat. Cover with cold water, bring to the boil and bubble for 5 minutes, drain and cool. Brown the meat well, a little at a time in the hot oil in a large flameproof casserole and drain from the fat. Add the onion, ground ginger and flour to the residual oil, fry gently for 3 minutes. Stir in the next six ingredients with the strained pineapple juice, seasoning and meat. Bring to the boil, cover and cook in the oven at 150°C (300°F) mark 2 for 1 hour. Add the pineapple chunks and pasta, re-cover and cook for a further 40 minutes, adjust seasoning.

Garnish with snipped parsley.

Suitable for freezing. Freeze without the pasta. Reheat in the usual way and add the pasta.

Lamb and Kidney Bean Casserole

125 g (4 oz) dried red kidney
    beans, soaked overnight
1 large breast of lamb
15 ml (1 tbsp) vegetable oil
450 g (1 lb) leeks, trimmed

400 ml (¾ pint) chicken stock
1 large garlic clove, skinned
    and crushed
salt and freshly ground
    pepper

bayleaf
125 g (4 oz) garlic sausage,
    in a piece

SERVES 4

Drain the beans and place in a saucepan. Cover with cold water and bring to the boil.
Boil rapidly for 10 minutes then simmer for a further 20 minutes. Drain again.
Meanwhile trim any excess fat off the lamb and chop into 5-cm (2-inch) pieces. Brown
well in the hot oil in a flameproof casserole, remove from the pan. Cut the leeks into
1-cm (½-inch) pieces, wash and drain well; lightly brown in the residual fat. Replace the
meat with the drained beans, bayleaf, stock, garlic, seasoning and bring to the boil. Cut
the sausage into fork-size pieces and add to the pan. Cover tightly and simmer gently
for about 1¼ hours. Serve with cauliflower sprigs or spinach.

*Suitable for freezing. Freeze without sausage. Reheat in the usual way and add sausage and finish
as above.*

Casserole of Spanish Lamb

800 g (1¾ lb) lean, boned
    lamb shoulder
45 ml (3 level tbsp) seasoned
    flour
30 ml (2 tbsp) vegetable oil
2.5 ml (½ level tsp) dried
    marjoram or mint

300 ml (½ pint) chicken stock
1 garlic clove, skinned and
    crushed
1 large green pepper, seeded
    and finely chopped
450 g (1 lb) potatoes, peeled
    and sliced thickly

4 sticks celery, finely chopped
25 g (1 oz) pimento-stuffed
    green olives, halved
4 medium tomatoes, skinned,
    seeded and quartered
salt and freshly ground
    pepper

SERVES 6

Cut the meat into 4-cm (1½-inch) cubes. Toss in seasoned flour. Heat the oil in a frying
pan or flameproof casserole and brown the meat on all sides. Blend in the stock, and
add marjoram, garlic, pepper and celery. If using a frying pan, transfer now to a
casserole. Cover and bake in the oven at 150°C (300°F) mark 2 for 1½ hours.

Add the potato slices to the casserole, cover and return to the oven for a further
¾–1 hour or until the potatoes are cooked.

To serve, stir in the olives and tomato quarters and adjust seasoning.

*Suitable for freezing. Freeze without potatoes, olives and tomatoes. Reheat in the usual way. Add
potatoes, olives and tomatoes and finish as above.*

Lamb with Apricots

125 g (4 oz) dried black-eye
   beans, soaked overnight
1.4 kg (3 lb) lamb shoulder,
   boned
salt and freshly ground
   pepper
1 medium onion, skinned
   and sliced

125 g (4 oz) mushrooms,
   wiped and sliced
30 ml (2 level tbsp) flour
2.5 ml (½ level tsp) chilli
   seasoning
15 ml (1 level tbsp) ground
   coriander
15 ml (1 tbsp) vegetable oil

600 ml (1 pint) chicken stock
45 ml (3 level tbsp) mango
   chutney
50 g (2 oz) dried apricots,
   soaked overnight
150 ml (¼ pint) natural
   yogurt
snipped parsley, to garnish

SERVES 4

Drain the beans and place in a saucepan. Cover with cold water, bring to the boil and boil rapidly for 10 minutes. Drain again. Cut the lamb into 2.5-cm (1-inch) cubes. Toss the meat in flour seasoned with chilli, coriander, salt and pepper; brown, a few pieces at a time, in the hot oil in a flameproof casserole. Remove from the fat, using a draining spoon. Add the onion and mushrooms and fry for a few minutes. Stir in the stock, beans, chutney, drained apricots. Replace the lamb. Bring to the boil, cover and cook in the oven at 170°C (325°F) mark 3 for about 1 hour until the meat is quite tender. Stir in the yogurt, adjust seasoning.

   Garnish with parsley.

Suitable for freezing. Reheat in the usual way.

Chilli Lamb and Coconut Curry

50 g (2 oz) desiccated coconut
200 ml (7 fl oz) milk
1.4 kg (3 lb) shoulder of
   lamb, boned
60 ml (4 tbsp) vegetable oil
1 medium onion, skinned
   and sliced

4 sticks celery
225 g (8 oz) cooking apples,
   skinned and sliced
2.5 ml (½ level tsp) chilli
   powder
5 ml (1 level tsp) ground
   cinnamon

60 ml (4 level tbsp) flour
400 ml (¾ pint) chicken stock
salt and freshly ground
   pepper
chopped parsley to garnish

SERVES 4

Bring the coconut to the boil in the milk and 200 ml (7 fl oz) water. Turn off the heat, leave to infuse for 30 minutes. Strain into a jug, pressing the coconut to extract all the juice.

   Cut up the lamb into 2.5-cm (1-inch) cubes and discard any excess fat. Brown in hot oil in a flameproof casserole and remove from the casserole. Cut the celery into 5-cm (2-inch) long pieces and brown with the onion and apple in the residual oil. Stir in the spices, flour, stock, coconut milk and seasoning and bring to the boil. Replace meat, cover and cook in the oven at 180°C (350°F) mark 4 about 1¼ hours. Garnish with parsley.

Suitable for freezing. Reheat in the usual way.

Pork

The pig gives us such a variety of meats — from the fragrant delicacy of pork fillet to the tangy saltiness of smoked bacon, not to mention the endless miscellany of sausages — that it is only understandable that there should be many ways of cooking pork and ham. There is very little waste on most cuts or joints of pork or bacon, and as all the meat is reasonably tender you can use any cut for your casseroles. The more economical cuts are belly, which has a delicious sweet flavour but is inclined to be fatty, hand or hock. Pork chops and fillets, though they do not require lengthy cooking, respond admirably to casseroling.

Any sweet-sour combination, such as apple or cider, red cabbage or prunes is successful with pork, the tart fruity flavours mingling perfectly with the richness of the meat.

Cassoulet

There are many recipes for this classic dish but the basic ingredients of the cassoulet are haricot beans, a well-flavoured pork sausage, and a piece of preserved goose. The latter can be bought canned, but if it is not available a perfectly good *cassoulet* can be made without it or other poultry can be substituted. This particular version, includes lamb as well as pork.

1 kg (2 lb) dried white haricot beans	2 onions, skinned and thinly sliced	450 g (1 lb) piece of coarse pork and garlic sausage
225 g (8 oz) salt pork or bacon, in one piece	3 garlic cloves, skinned and finely chopped	60 ml (4 tbsp) tomato purée
450 g (1 lb) loin or shoulder of pork, boned	1 small shoulder of lamb (or ½ large one), boned	1.75 litres (3 pints) water salt and freshly ground pepper
30 ml (2 tbsp) oil or fat from preserved goose	1 piece preserved goose (optional)	1 bouquet garni 100 g (4 oz) fresh breadcrumbs

SERVES 10–12

Rinse the beans in cold water, then put into a large saucepan. Cover with cold water, bring slowly to the boil and simmer for 5 minutes. Remove from the heat, cover and leave to soak in the water while you prepare the remaining ingredients.

Remove the rind from the salt pork or bacon, and from the pork, and cut it into small squares.

Heat the oil or goose fat in a large frying pan and fry the onions and garlic until softened. Add the pieces of rind and fry gently for 5 minutes. Raise the heat and brown on all sides, in turn, the pork and salt pork, the shoulder of lamb, the piece of goose and the sausage. Remove each from the pan when it is browned and set aside. Add the tomato purée to the pan with a little of the water, stir well to amalgamate any sediment and bring quickly to the boil.

Drain the beans, rinse them and put them in a clean saucepan with the remaining cold water. Bring to the boil, then pour the beans and water into the cassoulet pot. Add the contents of the frying pan, salt and pepper to taste and stir well. Bury the salt pork or bacon, the pork, the shoulder of lamb, the preserved goose and the sausage among the beans, add the bouquet garni, and bring to simmering point on top of the stove.

Sprinkle on a thick layer of breadcrumbs and place the cassoulet pot in the oven. Cook in the oven at 150°C (300°F) mark 2 for 2–3 hours. From time to time press down the crust which will have formed on top and sprinkle on a further layer of breadcrumbs. Tradition has it that the crust must be pressed down and renewed seven times, but after three times you should have a lovely golden crust. Larger pieces of meat should be cut up before serving.

Not suitable for freezing.

Baked Stuffed Pork Chops

50 g (2 oz) long grain brown rice	1 small onion, skinned and finely chopped	45 ml (3 tbsp) chopped parsley
4 spare rib pork chops	50 g (2 oz) seedless raisins	salt and freshly ground pepper
30 ml (2 tbsp) vegetable oil	226-g (8-oz) can pineapple	

SERVES 4

Cook the rice in plenty of boiling salted water for about 30 minutes until almost tender, drain well. Trim and bone the chops and brown well in the hot oil, cool. Slit three-quarters of the way through each chop to form a large pocket. Brown the onion in the residual oil. Stir in the raisins with the drained, chopped pineapple (reserving pineapple juice), cooked rice, parsley and seasoning. Place the chops in a shallow ovenproof dish. Use the rice mixture to stuff the prepared chops. Spoon round 60 ml (4 tbsp) seasoned pineapple juice. Cover the dish tightly and cook in the oven at 180°C (350°F) mark 4 for 1–1¼ hours. Baste once with the juice during cooking. Serve with carrots and brussels sprouts.

Suitable for freezing. Reheat in the usual way.

Gingered Spareribs with Apple

1.4 kg (3 lb) American pork
   spareribs
60 ml (4 tbsp) vegetable oil
450 g (1 lb) cooking apples,
   peeled and sliced
15 ml (1 level tbsp) flour

1 medium onion, skinned
   and sliced
7.5 ml (1½ level tsp) ground
   ginger
241-ml (8.5-fl oz) bottle dry
   ginger ale

400 ml (¾ pint) chicken stock
30 ml (2 tbsp) soy sauce
salt and freshly ground
   pepper
198-g (7-oz) can water
   chestnuts

SERVES 4–6

Cut up the meat into individual ribs, trimming off any excess fat. Brown well, a few at a time in hot oil in a large shallow flameproof casserole; remove from the fat. Fry the apples and onions in the residual fat for 2 minutes. Stir in the flour, ground ginger, ginger ale, stock and soy sauce and bring to the boil. Season to taste and replace the spareribs. Cover tightly and cook in the oven at 170°C (325°F) mark 3 for about 2 hours or until the meat is quite tender and readily comes away from the bone. Drain and halve the water chestnuts and stir into the casserole. Heat gently on top of the stove to warm through and skim off excess fat if necessary.

Not suitable for freezing.

Pork with Tomato and Barley

4 spare rib pork chops
30 ml (2 tbsp) vegetable oil
225 g (8 oz) onion, skinned
397-g (14-oz) can tomatoes

300 ml (½ pint) chicken stock
50 g (2 oz) pearl barley
large garlic clove, skinned
   and crushed

5 ml (1 level tsp) dried
   oregano
salt and freshly ground
   pepper

SERVES 4

Remove the bones and trim any excess fat off the chops. Divide each chop into three pieces. Brown well in the hot oil in a flameproof casserole and take out of the fat. Slice the onions into rounds and lightly brown in the residual fat. Add the contents of the can of tomatoes and the stock, barley, garlic, oregano and seasoning, bring to the boil. Replace the pork, cover tightly and cook in the oven at 170°C (325°F) mark 3 for about 1½ hours. Serve with baked jacket potatoes and cabbage wedges.

Suitable for freezing. Reheat in the usual way.

Osso Buco (see page 60)

Pork Loin with Cider

Ask your butcher to bone the pork, but to leave on the rind. Don't carve the joint until serving time — this helps to prevent it drying out.

600 ml (1 pint) dry cider	2 medium onions, skinned	125 g (4 oz) fresh
1.8 kg (4 lb) loin of pork, boned	50 g (2 oz) butter	breadcrumbs
	225 g (½ lb) button or cup	1 egg
salt and freshly ground pepper	mushrooms, wiped and chopped	175 g (6 oz) carrots, peeled
		30 ml (2 tbsp) vegetable oil
125 g (4 oz) rindless streaky bacon	5 ml (1 level tsp) dried rubbed sage	2 bayleaves
		15 ml (1 level tbsp) cornflour

SERVES 6

Pour the cider into a small pan and reduce by half. Remove the rind and most of the fat from the pork and cut into thin fingers. Place these in a small roasting tin, sprinkle generously with salt and set aside. Slit the pork along the eye of the meat three-quarters of the way through from the centre outwards. Open out to form a long roll.

Prepare the stuffing: chop one onion and snip the bacon into small pieces. Melt half the butter in a medium-sized frying pan, add the bacon and onion and cook slowly until the bacon fat runs and the ingredients begin to brown. Increase the heat, add the mushrooms and cook until all excess moisture has evaporated. Turn out into a large bowl, stir in the sage, breadcrumbs, egg and seasoning, mixing well, cool. Spread the cold stuffing over the pork, roll up and tie at regular intervals. Slice the carrot and the remaining onion. Heat the oil in a flameproof casserole, add the remaining butter and as it froths, brown the prepared joint well all over. Remove from the pan using draining spoons. Add the vegetables to the residual fat and lightly brown. Replace the meat and pour the reduced cider around. Stir in the bayleaves and seasoning and bring to the boil.

Cover tightly and place on a low shelf in the oven at 170°C (325°F) mark 3. Place the roasting tin of pork rind above and cook both for about 2¼ hours. Pierce the pork joint with a fine skewer, when done the juices should run clear. Lift the pork out of the casserole with any stuffing that may have oozed out and slice, discarding the string. Arrange on a serving dish, cover and keep warm in a low oven. Mix the cornflour to a smooth paste with a little water and stir into the pan juices. Bring to the boil, stirring all the time. Cook for 2 minutes, adjust seasoning then spoon the vegetables and juices over the meat. Serve with the crackling.

Not suitable for freezing.

Rognons Sauté Turbigo (see page 67)

Sausage and Bean Ragout

30 ml (2 tbsp) vegetable oil
450 g (1 lb) pork sausages or
    sausagemeat
175 g (6 oz) onion, skinned
    and sliced
125 g (4 oz) haricot beans,
    soaked overnight

125 g (4 oz) red kidney
    beans, soaked overnight
227-g (8-oz) can tomatoes
15 ml (1 level tbsp) cornflour
15 ml (1 level tbsp) chilli
    seasoning not chilli
    powder

30 ml (2 level tbsp) tomato
    purée
327-ml (11½-fl oz) can dry
    cider
salt and freshly ground
    pepper

SERVES 4

Heat the oil in a large flameproof casserole and brown the sausages or balls of sausagemeat well. Remove from the casserole and cut each sausage in half crosswise.

Put the onions in the casserole and fry until golden brown. Replace the sausages. Drain the beans and place in a pan. Cover with cold water, bring to the boil and boil rapidly for 10 minutes, then drain again. Add to the casserole with the tomatoes.

Blend the cornflour, chilli seasoning and tomato purée with a little cider until smooth, then stir in the remainder. Pour into the casserole.

Stir the casserole ingredients and mix well. Adjust seasoning. Cover tightly and cook in the oven at 170°C (325°F) mark 3 for about 2 hours or until the beans are tender.

Suitable for freezing. Reheat in the usual way.

Bacon Stew with Dumplings

900 g (2 lb) smoked bacon
    fore-end joint
450 g (1 lb) leeks, trimmed
    and washed
45 ml (3 tbsp) vegetable oil

45 ml (3 level tbsp) plain
    flour
400 ml (¾ pint) unseasoned
    stock
2 medium oranges

ground pepper
125 g (4 oz) self-raising flour
50 g (2 oz) shredded suet
45 ml (3 tbsp) snipped
    parsley

SERVES 6

Cut the bacon into 5-cm (2-inch) pieces, discarding the rind. Put it into a pan of cold water, bring to the boil and blanch for 1 minute. Drain and rinse under a cold tap. Slice the leeks, crosswise, into 1-cm (½-inch) pieces. Brown the bacon in the oil in a flameproof casserole. Stir in the plain flour, stock, finely grated rind and juice of one orange and bring to the boil. Add the leeks and season. Cover and cook in the oven at 170°C (325°F) mark 3 for 1¼ hours.

Mix remaining flour, suet and parsley with rind of the second orange. Bind with water to a firm but manageable dough and shape into six dumplings. Nestle dumplings in the casserole, replace the lid and cook in the oven for a further 40 minutes, or until the bacon is tender and the dumplings 'puffed up'. Garnish with remaining orange, segmented.

Suitable for freezing. Freeze without dumplings. Reheat in the usual way, add dumplings and finish as above.

Pork Ratatouille

450 g (1 lb) medium
  aubergines
6 medium sized pork chops
  about 700–900 g
  ($1\frac{1}{2}$–2 lb)
60 ml (4 tbsp) vegetable oil
225 g (8 oz) onions, skinned
  and sliced

450 g (1 lb) courgettes, sliced
350 g (12 oz) tomatoes,
  skinned and roughly
  chopped
150 ml ($\frac{1}{4}$ pint) dry white
  wine
1 large garlic clove, skinned
  and crushed

30 ml (2 level tbsp) tomato
  purée
5 ml (1 level tsp) dried
  oregano
salt and freshly ground
  pepper

SERVES 6

Wipe the aubergines and slice into 0.5-cm ($\frac{1}{4}$-inch) pieces, sprinkle with salt and leave to stand for 20 minutes; pat dry with absorbent kitchen paper. Meanwhile trim the chops, and flatten them slightly with the back of a knife, and brown well on both sides in the hot oil in a large frying pan. Drain the chops from the fat and place side by side in a shallow ovenproof casserole. The chops should just fit snugly into the casserole without too much space around. Add the onions and courgettes to the pan with the aubergines and fry over a high heat for a few minutes only to brown but still retain their shape. Add the tomatoes with the wine, garlic, tomato purée, herbs and seasoning and bring to the boil. Spoon over the chops, cover the dish tightly and bake in the oven at 170°C (325°F) mark 3 for about $1\frac{1}{4}$ hours, or until the chops are quite tender. Adjust seasoning and serve piping hot with rice.

Suitable for freezing. Reheat in the usual way.

Bacon in Cider

1.1 kg ($2\frac{1}{2}$ lb) smoked collar
  of bacon
4 cloves
300 ml ($\frac{1}{2}$ pint) dry cider
bayleaf

125 g (4 oz) fresh
  breadcrumbs
175 g (6 oz) self-raising flour
5 ml (1 level tsp) rubbed sage
50 g (2 oz) shredded suet

25 g (1 oz) margarine
175 g (6 oz) onion, skinned
salt and freshly ground
  pepper

SERVES 6

Place the bacon in a saucepan of cold water. Bring slowly to the boil. Drain off the water. Slice off the rind if it is not cooked enough to peel away. Stud the fat with cloves. Place the bacon in a shallow casserole with the cider and bayleaf. Cover tightly and cook in the oven at 180°C (350°F) mark 4 for about $2\frac{1}{4}$ hours.

Meanwhile combine the breadcrumbs, flour, sage and suet. Rub in the margarine. Coarsely grate in the onion and bind to a soft dough with water, season lightly. Shape into twelve dumplings.

Forty-five minutes before end of the cooking time add the dumplings to the juices surrounding the bacon. Cover again and finish cooking.

Not suitable for freezing.

Pork and Bacon Casserole

The crisply textured puff pastry fleurons contrast well with this rich casserole.

215-g (7½-oz) packet puff
   pastry, thawed
1 egg, beaten
1.1 kg (2½ lb) boneless chump
   end pork or pork fillet
100 g (4 oz) streaky bacon
30 ml (2 tbsp) vegetable oil
50 g (2 oz) butter

350 g (12 oz) button onions,
   skinned
60 ml (4 level tbsp) plain
   flour
600 ml (1 pint) chicken stock
finely grated rind of ½ lemon
salt and freshly ground
   pepper

30 ml (2 tbsp) fresh chopped
   sage or 5 ml (1 level tsp)
   dried
45 ml (3 tbsp) medium
   sherry
chopped parsley to garnish

SERVES 6

Ahead of time roll out the pastry to a 0.5-cm (¼-inch) thickness and brush with beaten egg. Stamp out crescents using a 6.5-cm (2½-inch) round cutter. Place on a greased baking sheet and bake in the oven at 220°C (425°F) mark 7 for about 15 minutes, cool on a wire rack. Cut up the pork into large bite-size pieces, discarding excess fat. Snip the rind off the bacon and divide into small pieces. Heat the oil and butter in a flameproof casserole and a little at a time, brown the pork and bacon well. Drain. Add the onions to the residual oil and lightly brown; mix in the flour and fry gently for 1–2 minutes.

Add the stock with the lemon rind, herbs and seasoning and bring to the boil, stirring, replace the meat. Cover the dish tightly and cook in the oven at 150°C (300°F) mark 2 for about 2 hours. Stir the sherry into the casserole and adjust the seasoning. Garnish the dish with puff pastry flowers and parsley.

Suitable for freezing. Freeze without sherry and pastry flowers. Reheat in the usual way.

Spring Pork Casserole

15 ml (1 tbsp) vegetable oil
4 pork spare rib chops,
   trimmed
1 medium onion, skinned
   and sliced

450 g (1 lb) new carrots,
   scraped
450 g (1 lb) potatoes, peeled
   and diced
300 ml (½ pt) chicken stock

2.5 ml (½ level tsp) mixed
   herbs
salt and freshly ground
   pepper
chopped parsley to garnish

SERVES 4

Heat the oil and quickly fry the chops on both sides until brown. Lift them out of pan. Add the onion and fry until golden. Combine the carrots, left whole if small, chunkily sliced if they are large, with the potatoes and place in a shallow casserole. Add the herbs and pour the stock over the vegetables. Lay the chops on the vegetables with the onion and season with salt and pepper. Cover and cook in the oven at 180°C (350°F) mark 4 for about 1 hour until chops are tender. Serve garnished with chopped parsley.

Suitable for freezing. Reheat in the usual way.

Tenderloin Casserole

900 g (2 lb) pork tenderloin
45 ml (3 tbsp) vegetable oil
25 g (1 oz) butter
350 g (12 oz) onions, skinned
and sliced
30 ml (2 level tbsp) flour
200 ml (7 fl oz) dry white
wine

450 g (1 lb) tomatoes,
skinned, quartered and
seeded
30 ml (2 level tbsp) tomato
purée
1 large garlic clove, skinned
and crushed
salt and freshly ground pepper

1 green pepper, halved,
seeded and thinly sliced
1 red pepper, halved, seeded
and thinly sliced
16 small black olives, halved
and stoned

SERVES 6

Cut the pork into 2-cm (¾-inch) chunks, discarding skin and excess fat. Heat the oil and butter in a large flameproof casserole and lightly brown the meat, half at a time. Remove from the pan and brown the onions. Stir in the flour with the tomatoes and their juices, the white wine, tomato purée, garlic and seasoning. Bring to the boil, replace the meat, cover and cook in the oven at 180°C (350°F) mark 4 for about 50 minutes, or until almost tender. Stir in the peppers and the olives. Return to the oven for about a further 20 minutes. Adjust seasoning and serve piping hot from the casserole.

Suitable for freezing. Freeze without peppers and olives. Reheat in the usual way and add peppers and olives.

Crumb Crusted Pork and Beans

125 g (4 oz) dried cannellini
beans, soaked overnight
700 g (1½ lb) belly of pork
450 g (1 lb) pork fillet
60 ml (4 tbsp) vegetable oil
225 g (8 oz) onion, skinned
and sliced

30 ml (2 level tbsp) flour
300 ml (½ pint) dry white
wine
397-g (14-oz) can tomatoes
5 ml (1 level tsp) dried basil
salt and freshly ground
pepper

10 ml (2 level tsp) sugar
225 g (8 oz) fresh brown
breadcrumbs
125 g (4 oz) Cheddar cheese,
grated
10 ml (2 level tsp) mustard
powder

SERVES 8

Drain the beans and place in a saucepan. Cover them with fresh water and simmer covered for 30 minutes. Remove the bones and skin from belly of pork. Cut belly and fillet into 4-cm (1½-inch) pieces. In a 2.8-litre (5-pint) flameproof casserole brown the meat a little at a time in the heated oil. Drain from the fat. Keep on one side. Brown the onion in residual fat, stir in the flour and cook for 1—2 minutes. Stir in wine, the contents of can of tomatoes, basil, sugar and seasonings. Bring to the boil, stirring. Add the drained cannellini beans and meat. Combine breadcrumbs, cheese and mustard. Sprinkle over the casserole. Cook, uncovered, in the oven at 170°C (325°F) mark 3 for about 1½ hours until tender and golden.

Not suitable for freezing.

Peanut Glazed Bacon Hock

1.1 kg (2½ lb) bacon hock
carrot, onion, bayleaf for
    flavouring
10 ml (2 tsp) lemon juice

30 ml (2 level tbsp) lemon
    marmalade
30 ml (2 level tbsp) demerara
    sugar

dash of Worcestershire sauce
25 g (1 oz) salted peanuts,
    chopped

SERVES 6

Place the bacon in an ovenproof casserole with some carrot, onion, bayleaf and enough water to come half-way up the joint. Cover and cook in the oven at 180°C (350°F) mark 4 for about 2¼ hours. Remove the bacon, carefully cut off the rind and score the fat. Combine the marmalade, sugar, lemon juice and Worcestershire sauce. Spread over the surface of the joint. Sprinkle on the chopped peanuts. Place joint in a roasting tin. Raise the oven temperature to 220°C (425°F) mark 7 and return joint to oven for a further 15 minutes to glaze.

Not suitable for freezing.

Nepalese Pork Curry

If you like your food on the hot side, leave the seeds in the red chillies.

700 g (1½ lb) blade of pork
45 ml (3 tbsp) vegetable oil
225 g (8 oz) onion, skinned
    and sliced
3 dried red chillies, seeded
    and finely chopped

10 ml (2 level tsp) ground
    cumin
5 ml (1 level tsp) ground
    cinnamon
15 ml (3 level tsp) ground
    coriander

2 garlic cloves, skinned and
    crushed
5 ml (1 level tsp) salt
ground pepper
150 ml (¼ pint) natural
    yogurt

SERVES 4

Cut up the pork into 3.5-cm (1½-inch) cubes, discarding skin, bone and excess fat. Brown the meat, a little at a time, in the hot oil in a large sauté pan; remove from the pan. Lightly brown the onion in the residual oil. Add the chillies to the pan with the spices and cook for 1 minute. Stir in 300 ml (½ pint) water with the remaining ingredients and bring to the boil. Replace the meat, cover the pan tightly and *simmer* for about 1¼ hours, or until the pork is tender. Adjust seasoning.

Suitable for freezing. Reheat in the usual way.

Braised Pork in Cider

4 loin pork chops, trimmed
50 g (2 oz) butter
30 ml (2 level tbsp) flour

300 ml (½ pint) dry cider
grated rind and juice of
1 lemon

salt and freshly ground
pepper
2 crisp green eating apples

SERVES 4

In a shallow flameproof casserole fry the chops in 25 g (1 oz) of the butter, remove from the pan and keep hot. Stir the flour into the butter and cook for 1 minute. Remove the pan from the heat and stir in the cider gradually. Simmer the sauce for 2–3 minutes until thickened, then add the lemon rind and the chops. Season to taste. Cover and simmer gently for 45 minutes, or until the meat is tender. Add the lemon juice.

Meanwhile remove the cores from the apples but do not peel them. Cut into 1-cm (½-inch) rings. Melt the remaining butter and sauté the apple rings quickly, until golden. Serve the pork garnished with apple rings.

Suitable for freezing. Freeze without apples. Reheat in the usual way and add apples.

Spicy Spare Rib Chops

4 spare rib pork chops
30 ml (2 tbsp) vegetable oil
1 large onion, skinned and
sliced
15 ml (1 level tbsp) cornflour
300 ml (½ pint) chicken stock
or water

30 ml (2 level tbsp) tomato
purée
5 ml (1 level tsp) mustard
powder
5 ml (1 level tsp) ground
ginger
15 ml (1 tbsp) vinegar

15 ml (1 tbsp)
Worcestershire sauce
15 ml (1 level tbsp) brown
sugar
15 ml (1 tbsp) lemon juice
salt and freshly ground
pepper

SERVES 4

Quickly fry the chops in the hot oil to brown. Drain and place in an ovenproof casserole. Fry the onion in the oil and add to the casserole. Blend the cornflour with a little of the stock and pour the remaining stock over. Pour into the pan, and heat gently, stirring, until it thickens. Mix together the remaining ingredients, stir into the sauce and pour into the casserole and cover. Cook in the oven at 170°C (325°F) mark 3 for about 1½ hours.

Suitable for freezing. Reheat in the usual way.

Cumberland Bacon

900 g (2 lb) boneless smoked
   bacon joint
15 ml (1 tbsp) vegetable oil
15 g (½ oz) butter
175 g (6 oz) onion, skinned
   and sliced
15 ml (1 level tbsp) French
   mustard

15 ml (1 level tbsp) flour
1 orange
300 ml (½ pint) chicken or
   ham stock
5 ml (1 tsp) wine vinegar
450 g (1 lb) potatoes, peeled
   and cut into 2.5-cm
   (1-inch) chunks

45 ml (3 level tbsp)
   redcurrant jelly
198-g (7-oz) can sweetcorn
   kernels, drained
1 medium green pepper,
   seeded and sliced
freshly ground pepper

SERVES 6

Remove rind and excess fat from the bacon and cut into 1.5-cm (¾-inch) cubes. Place in a saucepan of cold water and bring to the boil. Drain well. Heat the oil and butter in a flameproof casserole and soften the onion in it. Stir in the mustard and flour and cook for 1 minute. Finely grate in the orange rind, add 60 ml (4 tbsp) of juice, the stock, redcurrant jelly and vinegar. Bring to the boil, stirring. Blend in bacon, potatoes, sweetcorn, peppers and seasoning. Cover and cook in the oven at 180°C (350°F) mark 4 about 1¼ hours or until bacon is tender.

Suitable for freezing. Reheat in the usual way.

Chilli Sausage Casserole

450 g (1 lb) good quality
   sausagemeat
2.5 ml (½ level tsp) dried
   rosemary
2.5 ml (½ level tsp) dried sage
2.5 ml (½ level tsp) dried
   thyme
2.5 ml (½ level tsp) paprika
450 g (1 lb) green cabbage,
   trimmed and shredded

15 ml (tbsp) oil
1 large onion, skinned and
   sliced
213-g (7½-oz) can red
   kidney beans, drained
15 ml (1 level tbsp) chilli
   seasoning not chilli
   powder
1 garlic clove, skinned and
   crushed

30 ml (2 level tbsp) flour
150 ml (¼ pint) red wine
400 ml (¾ pint) beef stock
15 ml (1 level tbsp) tomato
   purée
15 ml (1 level tbsp) soft dark
   brown sugar
salt and freshly ground
   pepper

SERVES 4

Place the sausagemeat in a bowl and work in the dried herbs and paprika. With well-floured hands roll into 16 balls — about the size of golf balls. Heat the oil in a frying pan and fry the sausage until lightly browned. Drain well.

In a shallow 1.7-litre (3-pint) casserole layer up the cabbage, onion, kidney beans, and sausage. Blend chilli seasoning, flour and garlic into the pan residue, adding more oil if necessary, and cook for 1 minute. Stir in wine, stock, tomato purée, sugar and seasoning and bring to boil. Pour over ingredients in the casserole.

Cover tightly and bake in the oven at 180°C (350°F) mark 4 about 1 hour.

Suitable for freezing. Reheat in the usual way.

Pork and Corn Pan Supper

4 spare rib pork chops
30 ml (2 tbsp) vegetable oil
25 g (1 oz) butter
225 g (8 oz) onion, skinned
and sliced

45 ml (3 level tbsp) plain
flour
5 ml (1 level tsp) paprika
400 ml (¾ pint) chicken stock
198-g (7-oz) can corn niblets

salt and freshly ground
pepper
60 ml (4 level tbsp) natural
yogurt
chopped parsley to garnish

SERVES 4

Trim the meat away from the bones and slice into good fork-size pieces. Heat the oil and butter in a sauté pan and brown the meat well. Remove the meat from the pan. Add the onion and brown well, then stir in the flour and paprika and fry gently for 1 minute. Stir in the stock and bring to the boil, stirring. Season and add the drained corn niblets. Replace the pork. Cover the pan tightly and simmer gently for about 45 minutes, stirring occasionally. Stir the yogurt then blend it into the juices. Scatter with snipped parsley for serving.

Suitable for freezing. Freeze without yogurt. Reheat in the usual way and add yogurt.

Midweek Bacon Stew

100 g (4 oz) dried butter
beans, soaked overnight
700 g (1½ lb) bacon slipper
joint
225 g (8 oz) turnip, peeled
and coarsely diced

225 g (8 oz) parsnip, peeled
and coarsely diced
25 g (1 oz) lard
30 ml (2 level tbsp) flour
7.5 ml (1½ level tsp) mustard
powder

600 ml (1 pint) unseasoned
chicken stock
freshly ground pepper
chopped parsley to garnish

SERVES 6

Drain the butter beans and place in a pan. Cover with cold water, bring to the boil and boil rapidly for 10 minutes, then drain again.

Remove any rind from the bacon and cut the meat into 2.5-cm (1-inch) cubes. Place in a pan of cold water, bring to the boil and simmer for 5 minutes. Drain well.

Fry the vegetables gently in the hot fat in a flameproof casserole for 5 minutes. Stir in the flour and mustard, cook for 1 minute, then gradually stir in the stock. Stir until boiling.

Add the beans, meat and pepper. Cover and simmer gently for about 1½ hours until tender.

Suitable for freezing. Reheat in the usual way.

Sweet and Sour Pork with Peaches _____

450 g (1 lb) lean pork,
  minced
125 g (4 oz) fresh
  breadcrumbs
30 ml (2 tbsp) soy sauce
45 ml (3 tbsp) chopped
  parsley

salt and freshly ground
  pepper
1 egg
15 ml (1 level tbsp) cornflour
45 ml (3 tbsp) vegetable oil
3 medium onions, skinned
  and quartered

4 sticks celery
410-g (14½-oz) can peach
  slices
150 ml (¼ pint) chicken stock
30 ml (2 tbsp) white wine
  vinegar

SERVES 4 —————————————————————————————————

Combine the pork, breadcrumbs, soy sauce, parsley, seasoning and egg and roll into
sixteen balls. Flatten into patties. Coat the patties with cornflour and brown well in the
hot oil in a shallow flameproof casserole, then remove from the casserole. Replace with
the celery, cut into 5-cm (2-inch) sticks, and the onions. Brown lightly. Replace the
pork. Pour over the contents of the can of peaches, the stock and the vinegar. Bring to
the boil. Adjust seasoning, cover tightly and cook in the oven at 180°C (350°F) mark 4
for about 1 hour.

Not suitable for freezing.

Pot Roast of Pork and Red Cabbage _____

450 g (1 lb) red cabbage
45 ml (3 tbsp) red wine
  vinegar
15 ml (1 level tbsp) flour

225 g (8 oz) cooking apple,
  peeled, cored and sliced
15 ml (1 level tbsp) demerara
  sugar

salt and freshly ground
  pepper
700 g (1½ lb) boneless pork
  joint

SERVES 4 —————————————————————————————————

Shred the red cabbage and blanch in boiling water to which 15 ml (1 tbsp) vinegar has
been added and drain well. Place the apple with the cabbage in an ovenproof casserole
just wide enough to take the joint. Add the sugar, remaining vinegar, flour and
seasoning and stir well together. Slash the fat side of the joint several times and season
well. Place on top of the cabbage and cover the casserole. Cook in the oven at 190°C
(375°F) mark 5 for about 1¾ hours or until the pork is tender.

Not suitable for freezing.

Pork with Black Beans and Orange

350 g (¾ lb) streaky salt pork
30 ml (2 tbsp) vegetable oil
175 g (6 oz) onion, skinned
   and sliced
45 ml (3 level tbsp) flour

225 g (8 oz) carrots, peeled
   and sliced
600 ml (1 pint) chicken stock
1 bayleaf
1 orange

225 g (8 oz) black beans,
   soaked overnight
salt and freshly ground
   pepper

SERVES 4

Trim and dice the pork, fry in the hot oil in a flameproof casserole until golden. Add the onion and cook for about 3 minutes. Stir in the flour and cook for a few minutes. Add the carrot, stock and bayleaf along with a thinly pared strip of orange rind and 60 ml (4 tbsp) orange juice. Add the drained beans. Season well with salt and pepper, cover and simmer for about 1½ hours. Adjust seasoning and serve really hot.

Suitable for freezing. Reheat in the usual way.

Peppered Pork with Fruit

30 ml (2 level tbsp) whole
   black peppercorns
6 large pork chops
30 ml (2 level tbsp) flour

50 g (2 oz) butter or
   margarine
566-g (20-oz) can pineapple
   (small slices)

90 ml (6 tbsp) sherry
salt
12 cooked prunes

SERVES 6

Crush the peppercorns finely in a pestle and mortar or use the end of a plain rolling pin in a strong bowl or buy coarsely ground pepper. Trim the chops of excess fat and brown well in the hot fat in a large frying pan. Place side by side in a shallow ovenproof casserole. Drain the pineapple slices, reserve the juices and brown the slices a few at a time in the residual fat. Spoon over the chops. Stir the flour into the pan with the sherry, pineapple juice, crushed peppercorns and salt and bring to the boil. Stir in the drained prunes and spoon over the chops. Cover the dish tightly and cook in the oven at 180°C (350°F) mark 4 for about 50 minutes. Serve on shallow dish with juices spooned over.

Suitable for freezing. Reheat in the usual way.

Veal

Veal is a tender and delicate meat, since it comes from very young calves. It therefore needs very careful treatment, for if cooked too long the meat will disintegrate or dry out. As there is little or no fat, it is often sensible to add some bacon. Bacon also adds a delicate pink colour to the finished dish. Suitable cuts for casseroling are leg, shoulder, breast, neck or knuckle, or the trimmings usually sold as pie veal. The bones make excellent jellied stock which adds a delicious flavour to casseroles.

As the flavour is so mild most recipes call for more robust tastes to accompany the meat, such as tomato, ham, sausage or bacon, red or white wine, Marsala, soured cream or even cheese.

Veal is sometimes hard to come by or expensive, so most of these recipes would work equally well with tender cuts of pork.

Osso Buco

Ask your butcher for the hind shin, which is meatier and tastier than the front one, and get him to saw it into pieces about 6.5 cm (2½ inches) thick. *Osso Buco* is usually served with rice and followed with a green salad.

1 onion, skinned and very finely chopped	45 ml (3 level tbsp) flour salt and freshly ground pepper	5 ml (1 level tsp) grated lemon rind
65 g (2½ oz) butter		½ garlic clove, skinned and very finely chopped
15 ml (1 tbsp) vegetable oil	150 ml (¼ pint) dry white wine	
8 osso buco (veal shins), weighing about 1.75 kg (3½ lb), securely tied with string	300 ml (½ pint) beef stock 397-g (14-oz) can tomatoes, with their juice	15 ml (1 tbsp) chopped fresh parsley

SERVES 4 ———————————————————————— *Illustrated in colour opposite page 48*

In a flameproof dish, large enough to contain all the meat in a single layer and with a tightly fitting lid, gently fry the onion in the butter and oil for about 5 minutes, until soft.

Meanwhile coat the pieces of veal with the flour, shaking off any excess. Add the meat to the onion in the pan and brown well on both sides. Season with salt and pepper. Pour over the wine and boil rapidly for 5 minutes, turning the veal over several times. Add the stock and tomatoes, cover the saucepan and cook over very low heat for about 2 hours. Carefully turn and baste the veal bones every 15 minutes. If necessary add more stock during the cooking. If, by the time the meat is cooked, the sauce is too thin, remove the veal from the pan and reduce the liquid by boiling rapidly.

Mix together the lemon rind, garlic and parsley, to make the *gremolata*.

Remove the string from around the bones and serve piping hot with the sauce poured over the meat and the *gremolata* sprinkled on top.

Not suitable for freezing.

Veal Goulash with Caraway Dumplings

1.4 kg (3 lb) stewing veal
75 g (3 oz) lard
700 g (1½ lb) onions, skinned
   and sliced
450 g (1 lb) carrots, peeled
   and sliced
30 ml (2 level tbsp) plain
   flour

60 ml (4 level tbsp) paprika
900 ml (1½ pint) chicken
   stock
60 ml (4 tbsp) dry white
   wine
salt and freshly ground
   pepper
225 g (8 oz) self-raising flour

125 g (4 oz) shredded suet
10 ml (2 level tsp) caraway
   seeds
142 ml (5 fl oz) soured
   cream
75 ml (5 tbsp) water

SERVES 8

Cut up the veal into 4-cm (1½-inch) pieces. Brown it well, a little at a time in the hot lard; drain and place in a shallow ovenproof dish.

Lightly brown the onions and carrots, add the paprika and plain flour and fry for 2 minutes. Stir in the stock, wine and seasoning, bring to the boil and pour over veal.

Cover tightly and cook in the oven at 150°C (300°F) mark 2 for 2 hours.

Prepare sixteen dumplings from the flour, suet, caraway seeds, soured cream and water, seasoning well. Place on top of the goulash, sprinkle with extra caraway seeds. Bake in the oven at 170°C (325°F) mark 3 covered for about 30–40 minutes.

Not suitable for freezing.

Casserole of Rolled Stuffed Veal

2 kg (4½ lb) breast of veal
   with bone
75 g (3 oz) fresh
   breadcrumbs
125 g (4 oz) ham, very finely
   chopped
30 ml (2 tbsp) snipped chives

60 ml (4 level tbsp) soured
   cream
15 ml (1 level tbsp) whole
   grain mustard
25 g (1 oz) walnut pieces,
   chopped
30 ml (2 tbsp) white wine

salt and freshly ground
   pepper
450 g (1 lb) mushrooms,
   wiped and sliced
150 ml (¼ pint) white stock,
   preferably veal bone
parsley to garnish

SERVES 8

Trim all the fat from breast of veal and remove the bones.

Mix together the breadcrumbs, ham, chives, 30 ml (2 tbsp) soured cream, mustard, and walnuts.

Spread the stuffing mixture over the inside of the meat. Roll up the meat as tightly as possible and sew together with fine string or thick thread.

Place the mushrooms in the bottom of a flameproof casserole. Pour over the stock and wine and bring to the boil. Place the veal on top of the casserole, cover tightly, and cook in the oven at 150°C (300°F) mark 2 for about 3 hours.

Remove the meat from the casserole to slice for serving. Stir the remaining soured cream into the mushrooms and juices and boil to reduce for about 5 minutes. Pour over the veal. Garnish with snipped parsley.

Not suitable for freezing.

Hungarian Veal

700 g (1½ lb) tomatoes,
   skinned and sliced
1 large garlic clove, skinned
   and crushed
salt and freshly ground
   pepper

75 g (3 oz) butter
1.4 kg (3 lb) fresh spinach,
   cooked
700 g (1½ lb) fillet of veal
45 ml (3 tbsp) vegetable oil
60 ml (4 level tbsp) flour

7.5 ml (1½ level tsp) paprika
200 ml (7 fl oz) chicken stock
200 ml (7 fl oz) white wine
45 ml (3 tbsp) soured cream

SERVES 6

Fry the tomatoes and garlic in the butter for 1–2 minutes and place in the base of a shallow ovenproof dish. Spoon the seasoned chopped spinach on top.

Slice the veal into 7.5-cm (3-inch) long strips. Briskly fry a few at a time in the heated oil for 3 minutes each side and spoon on top of the spinach. Stir the flour and paprika into the pan juices, cook for 1 minute, stir in the stock and wine, simmer for 2 minutes. Season, cool slightly and whisk in the soured cream. Spoon the sauce over the veal and cover. Cook in the oven at 200°C (400°F) mark 6, for about 40 minutes.

Not suitable for freezing.

Fricassée of Veal

Add two cracked rib veal bones to the cooking liquor to give substance to the juices. Remove before finishing the sauce.

900 g (2 lb) stewing veal
450 g (1 lb) carrots, peeled
   and cut into fingers
125 g (4 oz) onion, skinned
   and sliced
150 ml (¼ pint) white wine

15 ml (1 tbsp) chopped fresh
   thyme or 2.5 ml
   (½ level tsp) dried
salt and freshly ground
   pepper
50 g (2 oz) butter

50 g (2 oz) flour
2 egg yolks
150 ml (¼ pint) single cream
snipped parsley to garnish

SERVES 6

Cut the veal into 4-cm (1½-inch) squares, discarding any skin and fat. Cover the meat with cold water, bring to the boil and bubble for 1 minute. Strain the veal through a colander and rinse under a cold tap to remove all scum. Rinse out the pan thoroughly and replace the meat. Add the carrots and onion to the pan with the herbs, wine, 900 ml (1½ pints) water and plenty of seasoning. Bring slowly to the boil, cover and simmer gently for about 1¼ hours, or until the veal is quite tender. Strain off the cooking liquor, make up to 700 ml (1¼ pints) with stock if necessary and reserve, keep the veal and vegetables warm in a covered serving dish. Melt the butter and stir in the flour, cook gently for 1 minute. Remove from the heat and stir in the strained cooking liquor; season well and bring to the boil, stirring all the time. Cook the sauce gently for 5 minutes. Mix the egg yolks with the cream, take the sauce off the heat and stir in the cream mixture. Return to the heat and warm gently – without boiling – until the sauce becomes slightly thicker; adjust seasoning. Pour the sauce over the meat. Garnish with snipped parsley for serving. Serve with soufflé potatoes and mushroom-stuffed tomatoes.

Not suitable for freezing.

Le Fricandeau

1.1 kg (2½ lb) boned shoulder
of veal
75 g (3 oz) larding bacon
50 g (2 oz) pickled pork,
rinded

1 medium onion, skinned
and finely sliced
75 g (3 oz) carrots, peeled
and finely sliced
bouquet garni

150 ml (¼ pint) dry white
wine
600 ml (1 pint) veal stock
salt and freshly ground black
pepper

SERVES 6

Cut the meat into slices about 3 cm (1¼ inch) thick; cut the bacon fat into thin strips and use to lard meat.

Place the pork in boiling water for 1–2 minutes. Drain and dice.

In a large deep flameproof casserole, scatter the pork and sliced vegetables over the bottom. Lay the pieces of veal in a single layer on these, threaded fat uppermost. Cover tightly. Place over heat to sweat for 15–20 minutes. Add wine and repeat for the same time. Repeat twice more with 150 ml (¼ pint) of stock each time. Do not allow the vegetables to brown.

Add the rest of the stock and the bouquet garni. Bring quickly to the boil, cover and cook in the oven at 150°C (300°F) mark 2 for about 2 hours; baste every 30 minutes.

Remove the meat from the casserole. Strain the gravy into a bowl, skim and return it to the clean casserole with the meat. Over a high heat cook rapidly until the liquid is reduced to 300 ml (½ pint). Adjust the seasoning. Place the meat on a serving dish and pour over the juices. Serve with puréed spinach.

Not suitable for freezing.

Ragout of Veal

900 g (2 lb) pie veal, cubed
45 ml (3 level tbsp) seasoned
flour
75 ml (5 tbsp) vegetable oil
16 button onions, skinned
396-g (14-oz) can tomatoes

175 g (6 oz) lean bacon
rashers, rinded and
roughly chopped
150 ml (¼ pint) dry white
wine
2.5 ml (½ level tsp) paprika

salt and freshly ground
pepper
113-g (4-oz) packet frozen
peas
45 ml (3 tbsp) soured cream
chopped parsley to garnish

SERVES 8

Toss the veal in seasoned flour and fry quickly in the hot oil. Remove to a large casserole or use a flameproof casserole at the start.

Add the bacon to the pan and fry with the onions for 3 minutes. Transfer to the casserole. Drain the tomatoes, chop them in half and add to the casserole with the wine. Season with paprika, and plenty of salt and pepper.

Cover and cook in the oven at 150°C (300°F) mark 2 for about 2¼ hours. Twenty minutes before the cooking is finished, stir in the peas and return to oven.

Beat the soured cream until runny and swirl over the casserole. Sprinkle with chopped parsley.

Suitable for freezing. Freeze without peas and soured cream. Reheat in the usual way, add peas and soured cream.

Offal

These delicious, nourishing and, with the exception of calves' liver, extremely economical parts of the animal are sadly so often badly cooked and unappetisingly served it is not surprising that many people malign liver, kidneys, hearts, sweetbreads or tripe. However, even the most conservative members of the family will be won over by these recipes, which bring out the rich, distinctive flavours of the meats.

All offal is very perishable and should really be eaten the day it is bought, or stored, unwrapped, in the refrigerator for no more than a day.

Mexican Liver

450 g (1 lb) lamb's liver
30 ml (2 level tbsp) seasoned
   flour
25 g (1 oz) butter or margarine
45 ml (3 tbsp) vegetable oil
2 onions, skinned and sliced

225 g (½ lb) tomatoes,
   skinned and sliced
1 red pepper, seeded and
   sliced
45 ml (3 level tbsp) plain
   flour

300 ml (½ pint) chicken stock
salt and freshly ground
   pepper
100 g (4 oz) long grain rice

SERVES 4

Wash the liver, slice it, toss it in seasoned flour, fry it lightly in the hot fat and oil for 5 minutes, then put it into a casserole. Fry the onions, tomatoes and red pepper (reserving a few slices of pepper) for 5 minutes and add to the liver. Stir the flour into the fat left in the pan and gradually add the stock; bring to the boil, stirring all the time, season well and pour over the liver. Cover and cook in the oven at 180°C (350°F) mark 4 for about 45 minutes. Meanwhile cook the rice in boiling salted water. Serve the liver on the rice and garnish with the sliced pepper.

Not suitable for freezing.

Lancashire Tripe and Onions

450 g (1 lb) dressed tripe
225 g (8 oz) shallots, skinned
salt and freshly ground
   pepper

568 ml (1 pint) milk
pinch of grated nutmeg
½ bayleaf (optional)
25 g (1 oz) butter

45 ml (3 level tbsp) flour
chopped parsley to garnish

SERVES 4

Simmer the tripe, shallots, milk, seasonings and bayleaf (if used) in a covered pan for about 2 hours, or until tender. Alternatively, cook in a casserole in the oven at 150°C (300°F) mark 2 for 3 hours. Strain off the liquid and measure 600 ml (1 pint). Melt the butter, stir in the flour and cook for 2–3 minutes. Remove the pan from the heat and gradually stir in the cooking liquid. Bring to the boil and continue to stir until it thickens. Add the tripe and shallots and reheat. Adjust the seasoning, sprinkle with parsley and serve with pieces of toast or boiled potatoes.

Not suitable for freezing.

Lambs' Hearts in a Casserole

8 lambs' hearts – about
175 g (6 oz) each
50 g (2 oz) butter or
margarine
1 medium onion, skinned
and chopped
125 g (4 oz) mushrooms,
wiped and chopped

125 g (4 oz) streaky bacon,
rinded and chopped
2.5 ml (½ level tsp) dried sage
or thyme
225 g (8 oz) fresh
breadcrumbs
finely grated rind of 1 lemon
1 egg, beaten

salt and freshly ground
pepper
60 ml (4 level tbsp) flour
30 ml (2 tbsp) vegetable oil
300 ml (½ pint) chicken stock
45 ml (3 tbsp) sherry

SERVES 8

Wash and trim the hearts and remove any ducts.

Heat half the butter in a frying pan. Lightly brown the onion, mushrooms and bacon. Remove from the heat and stir in the herbs, breadcrumbs, lemon rind and seasoning; bind with egg. Fill the hearts with the stuffing and sew up neatly. Toss the hearts in the flour and brown well in the remaining butter and oil in a flameproof casserole. Pour over the stock and sherry, season well and bring to the boil.

Cover the dish and cook in the oven at 150°C (300°F) mark 2 for about 2 hours, or until tender. Pour skimmed juices over the sliced hearts and serve.

Not suitable for freezing.

Casseroled Lambs' Hearts with Paprika

15 ml (1 tbsp) vegetable oil
225 g (8 oz) onions, skinned
and sliced
4 lambs' hearts, washed,
trimmed and thinly sliced
45 ml (3 level tbsp) flour

450 g (1 lb) carrots, peeled
and sliced
225 g (8 oz) parsnips, peeled
and sliced
15 ml (1 level tbsp) paprika
425-g (15-oz) can tomatoes

300 ml (½ pint) chicken stock
salt and freshly ground
pepper
8 slices French bread

SERVES 4

Heat the oil in a large saucepan or flameproof casserole and fry together the onion, hearts, carrots and parsnips for 10 minutes.

Add flour and paprika and fry for a further 2 minutes. Gradually stir in the tomatoes with their juice and the stock. Bring to the boil, stirring all the time.

Season well, and if needed transfer to a casserole. Cover and cook in the oven at 170°C (325°F) mark 3 for 2 hours.

Remove the lid, dip the slices of bread into the casserole juices and arrange them around the edge of the dish. Return to the oven, uncovered for 1 hour or until the heart is really tender.

Not suitable for freezing.

Stuffed Lambs' Hearts with Orange

4–6 lambs' hearts
75 g (3 oz) fresh
  breadcrumbs
25 g (1 oz) shredded suet
1 small orange

25 g (1 oz) gherkins, finely
  chopped
salt and freshly ground
  pepper
a little beaten egg to bind

225 g (8 oz) onions, skinned
  and thinly sliced
150 ml (¼ pint) beef stock

SERVES 4

Trim away any connective tissue from the hearts and snip with scissors to open out the cavity. Wash well.

Mix together the breadcrumbs, suet and gherkins, finely grate in the rind from the orange. Season well. Add just enough egg to bind together.

Stuff the hearts with the breadcrumb mixture, packing it in firmly. Sew them up with fine string or thread.

Arrange the onions in the base of a greased ovenproof dish large enough to take the hearts in a single layer.

Place the hearts on the bed of onions and pour over the orange juice and seasoned stock. Cover and cook in the oven at 180°C (350°F) mark 4 for about 1¼ hours. Remove the string, slice the hearts lengthwise and serve with the onion and juices.

Not suitable for freezing.

Ragout of Ox Heart with Lemon

450 g (1 lb) ox heart
25 g (1 oz) lard
1 medium onion, skinned
  and sliced
15 ml (1 level tbsp) flour
100 ml (4 fl oz) beef stock

finely grated rind of 1 small
  lemon
2.5 ml (½ level tsp) dried
  mixed herbs
salt and freshly ground
  pepper

5 ml (1 tsp) lemon juice
142 ml (5 fl oz) soured
  cream
15 ml (1 tbsp) chopped
  parsley

SERVES 4

Trim the heart, discarding any little pipes and gristle and cut into strips about 1 cm (½ inch) wide.

Melt the lard in a frying pan or a flameproof casserole and sauté the sliced onion until golden.

Fry the strips of heart quickly in the fat, to seal them on all sides.

Stir in the flour and cook for 1 minute, then gradually blend in the stock with the lemon rind, juice and herbs.

Bring to the boil and add salt and pepper to taste. Transfer to an ovenproof casserole if pan-fried. Cover and cook in the oven at 150°C (300°F) mark 2 for about 2 hours.

To serve, adjust seasoning, stir in the soured cream and sprinkle with freshly chopped parsley.

Not suitable for freezing.

Kidney and Sausage Ragout

700 g (1½ lb) lambs' kidneys
45 ml (3 tbsp) vegetable oil
450 g (1 lb) chipolata
   sausages
450 g (1 lb) carrots, peeled
   and finely sliced

225 g (8 oz) onions, skinned
   and finely sliced
60 ml (4 level tbsp) flour
600 ml (1 pint) beef stock
30 ml (2 level tbsp) tomato
   purée

45 ml (3 tbsp) brandy
salt and freshly ground
   pepper
1 large green pepper, diced
2 bayleaves

SERVES 8

Halve and skin the kidneys, snip out the cores. Brown well a few at a time in the hot oil in a large flameproof casserole. Remove from the pan with a draining spoon.

Add the sausages to the reheated pan juices and brown well all over, then take them out of the pan and halve each crosswise. Add the carrots and onions to the residual fat and fry to a golden brown. Stir in the flour, stock, brandy, tomato purée and seasoning and bring to the boil.

Replace the meats, add the pepper and bayleaves, cover tightly and bake in the oven at 150°C (300°F) mark 2 for about 40 minutes.

Remove the bayleaves just before serving and adjust the seasoning.

Not suitable for freezing.

Rognons Sauté Turbigo

15 lambs' kidneys
26 pickling onions
175 g (6 oz) butter
350 g (12 oz) mini pork
   sausages
45 ml (3 level tbsp) flour

350 g (12 oz) button
   mushrooms, halved
10–15 ml (2–3 tsp) tomato
   purée
45 ml (3 tbsp) sherry
600 ml (1 pint) beef stock

2 bayleaves
salt and freshly ground
   pepper
6 slices white bread
vegetable oil
chopped parsley to garnish

SERVES 6 — *Illustrated in colour opposite page 49*

Skin the kidneys, cut them in half lengthways and remove the cores. Pour boiling water over the onions, leave them 2–3 minutes, then drain and peel them. Heat a large frying pan with 25 g (1 oz) butter. Cook the sausages until they are brown on all sides and remove them from the pan. Wipe the pan clean, add 75 g (3 oz) butter and cook the onions and mushrooms over a brisk heat for 3–4 minutes, shaking the pan. Add to the sausages. Add the remaining butter, and when it is foaming, put in the kidneys and sauté briskly until they are evenly coloured (about 5 minutes). Add them to the sausages. Strain the fat and return it to the pan. Stir the flour, tomato purée, sherry and stock into the juices. Bring to the boil, stirring all the time. Add the bayleaves, seasoning and sausage and kidney mixture. Cover and simmer for 20–25 minutes.

Trim the bread into small triangles. Fry in oil until they are golden brown. Drain well and serve around the kidneys. Garnish with parsley scattered over the top.

Not suitable for freezing.

Tripe à la Mode de Caen

This famous dish can often be bought cooked and ready to serve in Normandy and large cities in France. It is usually of excellent quality because it is made in large quantities by first class specialists. Although it takes a long time to prepare, it is an easy dish to make.

1 kg (2 lb) dressed tripe	2 sprigs of parsley	600 ml (1 pint) cider or dry
1–2 cow heels	4 large onions, skinned	white wine
salt and freshly ground	4 cloves	60 ml (4 tbsp) Calvados
pepper	4 leeks, sliced and washed	(optional)
2 bayleaves	2 carrots, peeled and sliced	

SERVES 6

Wash the tripe very thoroughly and blanch it, then cut into small pieces. Divide up the cow heels. Place in a strong casserole with the tripe, seasoning, herbs, the onions (each with a clove stuck in it) and the leeks and carrots. Add the cider or wine and the Calvados (if used). Cover and cook in the oven at 150°C (300°F) mark 2 for 6 hours.

This dish may be left overnight. Remove the fat from the surface and take out the cow heel bones and the herbs before reheating for serving.

Not suitable for freezing.

Sweetbreads in Mushrooms and Cream

450 g (1 lb) lambs'	225 g (8 oz) mushrooms,	salt and freshly ground
sweetbreads	wiped and sliced	pepper
juice of 1 lemon	30 ml (3 tbsp) plain flour	bouquet garni
50 g (2 oz) butter or	150 ml (¼ pint) white wine	45 ml (3 tbsp) double cream
margarine	150 ml (¼ pint) chicken stock	

SERVES 4

Soak the sweetbreads in cold water and the lemon juice for 1 hour. Strain well. Remove any white tissue. Pat dry with absorbent kitchen paper.

Heat the butter in a flameproof casserole and add the sweetbreads until coloured lightly. Remove from the casserole and sauté the mushrooms in the remaining fat for 2 minutes. Add the flour and cook for 2 minutes. Pour in the wine and stock and replace the sweetbreads. Season lightly and add the bouquet garni. Cover and cook in the oven at 190°C (375°F) mark 5 for about 45 minutes until the sweetbreads are tender. Stir in the double cream before serving.

Not suitable for freezing.

Oxtail Paprika

2 oxtails, cut up – about 1.6 kg (3½ lb) total weight	30 ml (2 level tbsp) paprika	salt and freshly ground pepper
75 ml (5 tbsp) vegetable oil	60 ml (4 level tbsp) flour	142 ml (5 fl oz) soured cream
225 g (8 oz) onion, skinned and sliced	397-g (14-oz) can tomatoes 2 caps canned pimiento 600 ml (1 pint) beef stock	chopped parsley to garnish

SERVES 6

Trim the pieces of oxtail and brown well, a few pieces at a time, in hot oil in a large flameproof casserole; remove from the pan.

Brown the onion in the residual oil. Stir in the paprika and flour and cook gently for 1 minute.

Stir in tomatoes with their juice, sliced pimientos, stock and plenty of seasoning. Bring to the boil and replace the meat.

Cover the casserole tightly and cook in the oven at 170°C (325°F) mark 3 for about 3 hours or until the meat is really tender.

Shortly before serving, skim all fat from the surface of the casserole. Bring slowly to the boil, simmer gently for 10 minutes, covered. Remove from the heat and stir in the soured cream, then warm gently. Garnish with parsley.

Suitable for freezing. Freeze without the soured cream. Reheat in the usual way, add soured cream.

Curried Kidneys

450 g (1 lb) lambs' kidneys	15 ml (1 level tbsp) curry powder	salt and freshly ground pepper
50 g (2 oz) vegetable oil	45 ml (3 level tbsp) flour	50 g (2 oz) sultanas
2 large onions, skinned and sliced	600 ml (1 pint) beef stock or water	2 tomatoes, skinned and chopped
1 cooking apple, peeled and chopped	30 ml (2 tbsp) chutney	squeeze of lemon juice

SERVES 4

Peel, core and finely chop the kidneys. Fry the kidneys in the oil until brown. Drain well and put into a casserole. Fry the onions and apple in the fat remaining in the pan, and add to the meat. Fry the curry powder, add the flour and cook together for 2–3 minutes. Add the stock gradually and bring to the boil; add the seasoning and remaining ingredients and cook for 2–3 minutes, then pour over the meat. Cover the casserole and cook in the oven at 170°C (325°F) mark 3 for about 30 minutes. Adjust the seasoning as required and serve the curry with boiled rice.

Not suitable for freezing.

Lamb's Liver Bali Style

30 ml (2 tbsp) vegetable oil
1 medium onion, skinned
  and chopped
1 garlic clove, skinned and
  crushed
2.5 ml (½ level tsp) ground
  turmeric

2.5 ml (½ level tsp) soft
  brown sugar
30 ml (2 level tbsp) chopped
  salted peanuts
5 ml (1 level tsp) chilli
  seasoning not chilli powder
200 ml (7 fl oz) milk

450 g (1 lb) lamb's liver,
  sliced
1 bayleaf
salt and freshly ground
  pepper

SERVES 4

Heat the oil in a shallow flameproof casserole and sauté the onion and garlic for 2–3 minutes. Stir in the turmeric, sugar, peanuts, chilli seasoning and cook gently for 1 minute.

Add the liver slices to the casserole and seal quickly on both sides. Reduce the heat and stir in the milk. Add the bay leaf, salt and pepper to taste.

Cover and simmer very gently for about 30 minutes. If too much liquid remains, reduce slightly by gently boiling with the lid off.

Not suitable for freezing.

Baked Liver with Dumplings

350 g (12 oz) lamb's liver,
  sliced
1 medium onion, skinned
  and sliced
75 g (3 oz) celery, wiped and
  sliced

45 ml (3 tbsp) vegetable oil
225 g (8 oz) cooking apples,
  peeled and sliced
30 ml (2 level tbsp) plain
  flour
300 ml (10 fl oz) chicken stock

200 ml (7 fl oz) cider
salt and freshly ground
  pepper
125 g (4 oz) self-raising flour
50 g (2 oz) shredded suet
paprika to garnish

SERVES 4

Cut the liver into fork-size pieces and brown in the hot oil. Place in a shallow 1.7-litre (3-pint) ovenproof dish.

Brown the onion, celery and apples lightly in the residual oil.

Stir in the plain flour, stock, cider and seasonings, bring to the boil, cover and simmer for 20 minutes.

Mix self-raising flour, suet and seasoning, bind to a soft dough with water; shape into eight dumplings.

Pour the hot sauce over the liver and place the dumplings on top.

Cover the dish and bake in the oven at 190°C (375°F) mark 5 for about 40 minutes. Sprinkle with paprika for serving.

Not suitable for freezing.

Braised Oxtail

2 small oxtails cut up –
   about 1.4 kg (3 lb) total
   weight
30 ml (2 level tbsp) flour
salt and freshly ground
   pepper
40 g (1½ oz) lard

350 g (12 oz) onions, skinned
   and sliced
900 ml (1½ pints) beef stock
150 ml (¼ pint) red wine
15 ml (1 level tbsp) tomato
   purée
pared rind ½ lemon

2 bayleaves
225 g (½ lb) carrots, peeled
   and roughly chopped
450 g (1 lb) parsnips, peeled
   and roughly chopped
chopped parsley to garnish

SERVES 6

Coat the oxtails in the seasoned flour. Brown a few pieces at a time in the hot lard in a large flameproof casserole. Take them out of the pan.

Add the onions to the casserole and lightly brown. Stir in any remaining flour followed by the next five ingredients, and season well. Bring to the boil, and replace the meat.

Cover the pan and simmer for 2 hours; skim well.

Stir the carrots and parsnips into the casserole.

Re-cover the pan and simmer for a further 2 hours, or until the meat is quite tender.

Skim all the fat off the surface of the casserole. Bring slowly to the boil, simmer for 10 minutes, covered, adjust the seasoning and garnish with parsley.

Suitable for freezing. Reheat in the usual way.

Lambs' Tongues with Orange

700 g (1½ lb) lambs' tongues
   (about 4–6)
2 medium leeks
25 g (1 oz) butter or margarine

bouquet garni
½ chicken stock cube
30 ml (2 level tbsp) tomato
   purée

3 oranges
salt and freshly ground
   pepper

SERVES 4

Soak the tongues in cold water for 3–4 hours. Drain well.

Trim the leeks leaving about half the green part, slice them thinly, wash well and drain.

Melt the fat in a flameproof casserole and sauté the leeks for 5 minutes. Off the heat, add the bouquet garni, crumbled stock cube, tomato purée and the juice of 1 orange made up to 150 ml (¼ pint) with water.

Peel two strips from orange rind free of white pith. Place with the tongues in the casserole. Cover closely, bring to the boil, reduce heat and simmer for about 1½ hours until the tongues are tender.

Remove the tongues from the casserole, skin them and cut them into strips. Discard bouquet garni and orange peel. Return to the casserole, adjust the seasoning and bring to serving temperature. Garnish with segments cut from the other two oranges.

Not suitable for freezing.

Eastern Spiced Liver

25 g (1 oz) desiccated coconut
350 g (12 oz) lamb's liver
45 ml (3 tbsp) vegetable oil
25 g (1 oz) butter or
  margarine
225 g (8 oz) onion, skinned
  and sliced
5 ml (1 level tsp) paprika

15 ml (3 level tsp) chilli
  seasoning not chilli powder
15 ml (3 level tsp) ground
  coriander
2.5 ml ($\frac{1}{2}$ level tsp) ground
  turmeric
30 ml (2 level tbsp) plain
  flour

400 ml ($\frac{3}{4}$ pint) chicken stock
30 ml (2 level tbsp) mango
  chutney
salt and freshly ground
  pepper
lemon twists and poppadums
  to accompany

SERVES 4

Soak the coconut in 150 ml ($\frac{1}{4}$ pint) boiling water for 15 minutes, strain, reserving the juices.

Slice the liver into large fork-size pieces and in a shallow flameproof casserole brown well in a mixture of hot oil and butter, then take out of the pan. Add the onion to the pan and fry until golden; stir in the spices and flour and cook for 1 minute, stirring. Add the stock with the coconut 'milk', chutney and seasoning and bring to the boil. Replace the liver, cover and simmer for 15–20 minutes. Garnish with lemon twists and poppadums.

Suitable for freezing. Reheat in the usual way on top of the stove.

Baked Kidney Risotto

1 medium onion, skinned
  and chopped
25 g (1 oz) butter
325 g (12 oz) lambs' kidneys

1 medium green pepper,
  seeded and roughly
  chopped
400 ml ($\frac{3}{4}$ pint) chicken stock

30 ml (2 tbsp) sherry
225 g (8 oz) long grain rice
2.5 ml ($\frac{1}{2}$ level tsp) turmeric

SERVES 4

Soften the onion in the butter in a sauté pan, add the green pepper and cook till lightly brown.

Skin, halve the kidneys, remove the cores and cut into strips. Add to ingredients in the pan and cook stirring, until browned. Transfer to 1.7 litre (3 pint) casserole.

Add seasoned stock and sherry to the pan, bring to the boil and shower in the rice. Cover and simmer for 5 minutes. Stir in the turmeric and add all this to the casserole.

Cover casserole and cook in the oven at 170°C (325°F) mark 3 for 30–35 minutes or until the rice is tender and the stock absorbed – the rice should be moist but not dry.

Not suitable for freezing.

Liver and Sausage Casserole

225 g (8 oz) pork chipolata
    sausages
225 g (8 oz) lamb's liver,
    sliced
225 g (8 oz) small onions,
    skinned and quartered

30 ml (2 tbsp) vegetable oil
30 ml (2 level tbsp) plain
    flour
400 ml (¾ pint) chicken stock
15 ml (1 level tbsp) French
    mustard

salt and freshly ground
    pepper
30 ml (2 tbsp) sherry
    (optional)

SERVES 4

Heat the oil in a large shallow flameproof casserole and brown the sausages, add the liver and quickly brown. Drain it from the fat.

Brown the onions lightly in the residual oil; stir in the flour and fry gently for 1–2 minutes. Mix in the stock, mustard and seasoning and bring to the boil. Replace the liver and the halved sausages. Cover the pan tightly and simmer gently for about 15 minutes, or until the meat and vegetables are just tender.

Adjust the seasoning and stir in the sherry for serving.

Suitable for freezing. Freeze without sherry. Reheat in the usual way on top of the stove.

Liver in Yogurt with Cucumber

450 g (1 lb) sliced lamb's
    liver
30 ml (2 level tbsp) flour
2.5 ml (½ level tsp) dried
    thyme
45 ml (3 tbsp) vegetable oil

salt and freshly ground
    pepper
150 ml (¼ pint) chicken stock
20 ml (4 level tsp) Dijon
    mustard
1 small cucumber

150 ml (¼ pint) natural
    yogurt
1 small green pepper
1 large onion, skinned
25 g (1 oz) butter

SERVES 4

Cut the liver into strips about 6 cm (2½ inch) long by 1 cm (½ inch) wide.

Mix the flour, thyme and seasoning together. Toss the liver in the flour mixture and brown in the hot oil in a shallow flameproof casserole. Stir in the stock and mustard and bring to the boil. Peel the cucumber and cut into small fingers, discarding the seeds. Stir into the casserole with the yogurt. Cover and cook in the oven at 170°C (325°F) mark 3 for about 30 minutes until tender.

Meanwhile seed, thinly slice and blanch the pepper. Thinly slice the onion into rings, fry in the butter with the pepper until golden. Use as a garnish.

Not suitable for freezing.

Poultry & Game

Poultry – the chickens, capons, ducks and turkeys bred specifically for food – offers an incredible variety of dishes. They are all fed on standard poultry feeds and their tastes differ little, unless you can manage to obtain free-range birds for eating. Like their eggs, free-range birds taste better than their battery-reared counterparts, and their flesh is far firmer. There is also a noticeable difference in taste between frozen and fresh poultry.

Game on the other hand, refers to wild birds or animals, though many game birds are now reared in captivity before being sold to gamekeepers to ensure plenty of sport for the increasingly popular shooting syndicates. They do have a brief life of freedom in the wild however, and fending for themselves on the moors or in the woods means that their flavour is no less distinctive than the genuinely wild game birds.

Game birds and animals are protected by law and can only be killed at certain times of the year, usually through autumn and early winter. Rabbit and pigeon are treated here as game, as they are usually prepared as game, though they have no closed season. Tame rabbit is frequently available in butchers, though the flavour of fresh wild rabbit is quite a different matter. Most game is available at poulterers and good fishmongers, and many supermarkets now sell ready-prepared pheasant, partridge and other game birds.

Poultry

All poultry is extremely versatile and responds perfectly to any form of casseroling. Surely the chicken must be the subject of more recipes throughout the world than any other meat – every country has its speciality – and included here are unusual dishes from as widely diverse countries as Morocco and Japan, though the classic Coq au Vin has not been forgotten.

Boiling fowls, tasty mature hens which naturally require long slow cooking, are ideal for casseroles though fresh and frozen roasting birds are equally good. Now that turkey pieces are widely available at very reasonable prices we can also experiment with this succulent meat that was formerly saved for special occasions. In the same way, duck is also very easily accessible, and provides a variety of tasty dishes.

Chicken Supremes in Wine and Cream

Ask the butcher to prepare the supremes French-style with the wing bone attached. Chicken breast fillets can be used and, when in season, 75 g (3 oz) shallots substituted for the onion.

6 chicken supremes (about
175 g (6 oz) each)
1 small onion, skinned
225 g (½ lb) tomatoes,
skinned
45 ml (3 tbsp) red wine
vinegar

50 g (2 oz) unsalted butter
15 ml (1 level tbsp) tomato
purée
1 large garlic clove, skinned
and crushed
150 ml (5 fl oz) dry white
wine

300 ml (½ pint) chicken stock
salt and freshly ground
pepper
150 ml (¼ pint) double cream
chopped parsley to garnish

SERVES 6

Wipe the chicken and trim any excess skin. Finely chop the onion and roughly chop the tomatoes. Place the vinegar in a small saucepan and reduce by half. Heat the butter in a flameproof casserole. Well brown the chicken pieces on all sides and remove from the pan with a slotted spoon. Add the onion, tomatoes, tomato purée and garlic, cover and cook gently for about 5 minutes to soften the onions a little. Add the wine and cook, uncovered, over a high heat until the wine reduces by half. Add the vinegar, stock and seasoning and bring to the boil. Replace the chicken, covering it with the sauce. Simmer gently, covered, for about 25 minutes, or until the chicken is quite tender. Lift the chicken out of the pan with a slotted spoon and keep warm. Reduce the sauce by half, then stir in the cream. Continue reducing the sauce until a thin pouring consistency is obtained. Adjust seasoning, pass through a strainer and spoon over the chicken for serving. Garnish with chopped parsley.

Not suitable for freezing.

Chicken with Mint

4 chicken quarters, halved
and skinned, 900 g (2 lb)
total weight
900 g (2 lb) potatoes, peeled
and thinly sliced

25 g (1 oz) butter
225 g (8 oz) leeks, washed
and roughly sliced
10 ml (2 level tsp) dried mint
15 ml (1 level tbsp) flour

60 ml (4 tbsp) chicken stock
salt and freshly ground
pepper
chopped parsley to garnish

SERVES 4

Heat the butter in a large frying pan, add the chicken and brown well in the melted butter. In a deep, buttered 1.7-litre (3-pint) casserole, layer the potato, chicken and leeks with the mint and flour; season well between each layer. Finish with a layer of potato. Pour over the stock.

Cover tightly. Bake in the oven at 170°C (325°F) mark 3 for 1 hour. Uncover and cook for about a further 30 minutes to brown the top. Serve garnished with chopped parsley.

Not suitable for freezing.

Chicken with Vermouth and Olives

8 chicken thighs, skinned —
   about 900 g (2 lb)
40 g (1½ oz) seasoned flour
50 g (2 oz) butter
150 ml (¼ pint) dry vermouth
   or white wine

1 small garlic clove, skinned
   and crushed
142 ml (5 fl oz) soured
   cream
50 g (2 oz) black olives,
   stoned and sliced

300 ml (½ pint) chicken stock
salt and freshly ground
   pepper
flaky pastry scraps and
   parsley sprigs to garnish

SERVES 4   *Illustrated in colour opposite page 80*

Toss the chicken thighs in seasoned flour. In a flameproof casserole melt the butter and brown the chicken well all over. Remove from the fat and put aside.

Stir in remaining seasoned flour, cook for 2–3 minutes. Gradually stir in the stock, vermouth and crushed garlic. Boil for 2–3 minutes, stirring.

Replace the chicken, cover and simmer gently for about 1 hour.

Remove the chicken pieces to a serving dish and keep warm.

Stir the soured cream into the pan juices. Heat gently for 3–4 minutes, without boiling. Just before serving add the olives. Adjust seasoning and spoon the sauce over the chicken. Garnish with pastry crescents and parsley.

For garnish, cut pastry scraps into crescents, bake in the oven at 220°C (425°F) mark 7 for about 12 minutes.

Not suitable for freezing.

Chicken and Stilton Roulades

125 g (4 oz) Stilton cheese,
   crumbled
75 g (3 oz) unsalted butter,
   softened
4 chicken breasts, skinned
   and boned

8 rashers smoked back bacon
15 ml (1 tbsp) vegetable oil
25 g (1 oz) butter
1 glass red wine made up to
   300 ml (½ pint) with
   chicken stock

5 ml (1 level tsp) arrowroot
salt and freshly ground
   pepper
watercress for garnish

SERVES 4

Cream Stilton and unsalted butter to a smooth paste.

Bat out chicken breasts between two sheets of damp greaseproof paper. Spread Stilton butter evenly on one side of each breast.

Roll up the chicken breasts and wrap them in rinded bacon rashers. Secure each with a cocktail stick.

In a flameproof casserole heat the oil and butter and brown the chicken rolls well.

Pour in red wine and stock, season, bring to the boil, cover and simmer very gently for 35–40 minutes, turning occasionally. Remove the meat to serving dish and keep it warm.

Thicken the pan juices with a smooth paste of arrowroot and water in the usual way. Season. Spoon sauce over meat. Garnish with watercress sprigs.

Not suitable for freezing.

Coq au Vin

1 large roasting chicken or
    capon, jointed, or 6 to
    8 chicken joints
30 ml (2 level tbsp) flour
salt and freshly ground
    pepper
100 g (4 oz) lean bacon,
    diced
1 onion, skinned and
    quartered

90 g (3½ oz) butter
1 carrot, peeled and
    quartered
60 ml (4 tbsp) brandy
600 ml (1 pint) red
    burgundy wine
1 garlic clove, skinned and
    lightly crushed
1 bouquet garni
1 sugar lump

30 ml (2 tbsp) vegetable oil
450 g (1 lb) small onions,
    skinned
pinch of sugar
5 ml (1 tsp) wine vinegar
225 g (8 oz) button
    mushrooms
6 slices of white bread, crusts
    removed

SERVES 6–8

Coat the chicken pieces with 15 ml (1 tbsp) of the flour, liberally seasoned with salt and pepper.

Melt 25 g (1 oz) of the butter in a flameproof casserole, add the bacon, onion and carrot and fry gently until the bacon begins to change colour. Add the chicken pieces, raise the heat and fry until they are golden brown on all sides.

Heat the brandy in a small saucepan, set it alight and pour over the chicken, shaking the pan so that all the chicken pieces are covered in flames. When the flames have subsided, pour on the wine and stir to remove any sediment from the bottom of the casserole. Add the garlic, bouquet garni and sugar lump. Bring to the boil, then cover and simmer very gently for 1–1½ hours until the chicken is tender. Test by pricking the thickest part of a drumstick; the chicken is done when the juice runs out clear.

Meanwhile, melt another 25 g (1 oz) of the butter with 7.5 ml (½ tbsp) of the oil in a frying pan. Add the small onions and fry until they begin to brown. Add the pinch of sugar and the vinegar, together with 15 ml (1 tbsp) of the chicken cooking liquid. Cover and simmer for 10–15 minutes or until just tender. Keep warm.

Melt 25 g (1 oz) of the butter with 7.5 ml (½ tbsp) of the oil in a heavy saucepan that is wide enough to hold the mushrooms lying flat. Raise the heat and add the mushrooms. Cook until they are crisp and lightly browned. Keep warm.

When cooked, lift the chicken pieces out of the casserole and place in a deep heated serving dish. Surround with the small onions and mushrooms and keep hot.

Discard the bouquet garni. Skim the excess fat off the cooking liquid and put it into a frying pan. Boil the liquid in the casserole briskly to reduce for 3–5 minutes.

Add the remaining oil to the fat in the frying pan and quickly fry the pieces of bread until golden brown on both sides. Cut each slice into triangles.

Work the remaining flour into the remaining butter to make 'beurre manié'. Take the casserole off the heat and add the beurre manié in small pieces to the cooking liquid. Stir until smooth, then bring just to the boil. The sauce should now be quite thick and shiny. Adjust the seasoning and pour over the chicken. Garnish with the triangles of fried bread.

Serve with a green salad.

Suitable for freezing. Freeze after the simmering of the chicken. Reheat in the usual way and continue as above.

Chicken Hot Pot

1.4 kg (3 lb) oven-ready
  chicken
700 g (1½ lb) floury potatoes,
  peeled
439-g (15½-oz) can butter
  beans

225 g (½ lb) leeks
salt and freshly ground
  pepper
400 ml (¾ pint) chicken stock
10 ml (2 level tsp) Dijon
  mustard

15 ml (1 level tbsp) tomato
  purée
25 g (1 oz) butter
chopped parsley to garnish

SERVES 4

Remove all the flesh from chicken and discard the skin and bone. Dice into 2.5-cm (1-inch) pieces, including any scraps.

Slice the leeks, discarding the dark green leaves and wash well. Slice the potatoes into thick matchsticks.

Layer up the chicken, leeks and drained beans with one-third of the potatoes in the centre using a 2.4-litre (4½-pint) ovenproof casserole. Season each layer well.

Mix the stock with mustard and tomato purée, pour into the dish. Top with remaining potatoes, dot with butter. Cover and bake in the oven at 180°C (350°F) mark 4 for about 1 hour until potatoes are tender.

Uncover and return to oven at 220°C (425°F) mark 7 for about 30 minutes, until golden and crisp.

Sprinkle with parsley for serving.

Suitable for freezing. Reheat in the usual way.

Chicken Molé

50 g (2 oz) butter
1.8 kg (4 lb) oven-ready
  chicken, jointed
5 ml (1 level tsp) salt
400 ml (¾ pint) chicken stock
1 green pepper, seeded and
  chopped
2.5 ml (½ level tsp) aniseed

15 ml (1 level tbsp) sesame
  seeds
2 garlic cloves, skinned and
  crushed
pinch of ground cloves
pinch of ground cinnamon
pinch of black pepper
3 tomatoes, skinned

1.25 ml (¼ level tsp) whole
  coriander
2 squares unsweetened dark
  chocolate, grated
45 ml (3 level tbsp) ground
  almonds
2.5 ml (½ level tsp) chilli
  powder

SERVES 4

Melt the butter and brown the chicken joints on all sides. Drain and place in an ovenproof casserole.

Place all the remaining ingredients in a blender and blend until smooth.

Pour the sauce over the chicken and cover. Bake in the oven at 180°C (350°F) mark 4 for 1–1½ hours until the chicken is tender.

Note 15–30 ml (1–2 level tbsp) chilli seasoning can be used to replace the chilli powder.

Suitable for freezing. Reheat in the usual way.

Chicken and Watercress Casserole

1 large bunch of watercress
1.4 kg (3 lb) oven ready
  chicken
15 g (½ oz) butter
15 ml (1 tbsp) vegetable oil

2 medium onions, skinned
  and sliced
100 g (4 oz) frozen peas
salt and freshly ground
  pepper

200 ml (7 fl oz) chicken stock
60 ml (4 tbsp) soured cream
croûtons of fried bread to
  garnish

SERVES 6 —————————————————————— *Illustrated in colour opposite page 81*

Trim, wash and chop the watercress, keeping a little for the garnish.

Joint the chicken into eight pieces, leaving the skin on, and brown well in the melted butter and oil in a shallow flameproof casserole. Remove from the casserole.

Add the onion to the residual fat and cook until soft. Stir in the watercress and cook, stirring for 2 minutes. Return the chicken to the pan with the frozen peas.

Pour over the stock and add the seasoning. Cover tightly and bake in the oven at 180°C (350°F) mark 4 for about 1 hour, until the chicken is tender.

Remove the chicken and keep warm. Purée the cooking liquid in a blender, return it to the casserole and bring to the boil. Stir the soured cream, then add to the sauce off the heat.

Spoon the sauce over the chicken and serve garnished with croûtons.

Not suitable for freezing.

Chicken with Peanuts and Raisins

1.4 kg (3 lb) oven-ready
  chicken
30 ml (2 level tbsp) seasoned
  flour
30 ml (2 tbsp) vegetable oil

2 medium onions, skinned
  and sliced into rings
15 ml (1 level tbsp) smooth
  peanut butter
200 ml (7 fl oz) chicken stock

25 g (1 oz) seedless raisins
25 g (1 oz) peanuts
45 ml (3 tbsp) single cream

SERVES 4 —————————————————————————————————

Joint the chicken into eight pieces, coat them in seasoned flour and brown well on all sides in the oil. Drain and transfer to a flameproof casserole.

In the oil residue fry the onion rings until golden and scatter over the chicken.

Stir the remaining flour and the peanut butter into the frying pan, scraping any sediment from the bottom. Slowly stir in the stock and bring to the boil. Season well. Pour over the chicken and sprinkle raisins on top.

Cover the casserole, cook in the oven at 180°C (350°F) mark 4 for about 1 hour, until the chicken is tender.

Serve sprinkled with peanuts; spoon the cream over the top.

Suitable for freezing. Freeze without peanuts and cream. Reheat in the usual way. Then add garnish.

Chicken with Vermouth and Olives (see page 77)

Gingered Japanese Chicken

1.4 kg (3 lb) oven ready
  chicken
15 ml (1 level tbsp) flour
15 ml (1 level tbsp) ground
  ginger
60 ml (4 tbsp) vegetable oil

1 medium onion, skinned
  and sliced
1 red pepper
283-g (10-oz) can bamboo
  shoots
150 ml (¼ pint) chicken stock

45 ml (3 tbsp) soy sauce
45 ml (3 tbsp) medium dry
  sherry
salt and freshly ground
  pepper
125 g (4 oz) cup mushrooms

SERVES 4

Cut all the flesh off the chicken and slice into chunky 'fingers', discarding the skin. Mix the flour and ginger together on a sheet of greaseproof paper or in a polythene bag and toss the chicken in it.

Heat the oil in a large flameproof casserole and fry the chicken and onion together until golden.

Halve, seed and slice the pepper; cut up the bamboo shoots into 1-cm (½-inch) strips; add both to the casserole.

Stir in the stock, soy sauce, sherry and seasoning. Bring to the boil. Cover and simmer for 15 minutes.

Add the sliced mushrooms, cover again and cook for a further 5–10 minutes, or until the chicken is tender.

Suitable for freezing. Freeze without mushrooms. Reheat in the usual way and add mushrooms.

Spring Chicken Casserole

1 small chicken – about
  1.1 kg (2½ lb)
25 g (1 oz) lard
397-g (14-oz) can tomatoes
450 g (1 lb) small carrots,
  peeled

1 medium onion, skinned
  and sliced
45 ml (3 level tbsp) flour
600 ml (1 pint) chicken stock
salt and freshly ground
  pepper

150 g (5 oz) self-raising flour
75 g (2½ oz) shredded suet
finely grated rind ½ lemon
30 ml (2 tbsp) chopped
  parsley

SERVES 3–4

Cut chicken into eight pieces. Remove the skin, trim away bones and use them for stock. Fry quickly in hot lard to brown evenly. Transfer to a 1.7-litre (3-pint) ovenproof casserole.

Drain the juice from the tomatoes and reserve. Nestle tomatoes and halved carrots between the chicken pieces.

Fry the onion quickly in pan fat and stir in the flour; slowly add stock and tomato liquid, cook to thicken, stirring. Season and add to the casserole.

Cover and cook in the oven at 190°C (375°F) mark 5 for about 50 minutes.

Combine flour, pinch of salt, suet, rind, parsley and cold water into a light dough; form eight balls and add to the casserole. Bake for a further 20 minutes.

Suitable for freezing. Freeze without dumplings. Reheat in the usual way and add dumplings and continue as above.

Chicken and Watercress Casserole (see page 80)

Pot Roast Chicken with Onion Sauce

450 g (1 lb) onion, skinned
liver from the chicken
25 g (1 oz) walnut pieces
25 g (1 oz) margarine
225 g (8 oz) fresh
   breadcrumbs
30 ml (2 tbsp) lemon juice

30 ml (2 tbsp) chopped
   parsley
25 g (1 oz) coarse oatmeal
25 g (1 oz) shredded suet
1½-kg (3-lb) oven-ready
   chicken
oil for frying

salt and freshly ground
   pepper
300 ml (½ pint) milk
bayleaf
15 ml (1 level tbsp) cornflour

SERVES 4

Finely chop the onion, liver and walnuts. Sauté 225 g (8 oz) onion, the liver and walnuts in the margarine for 3–4 minutes. Mix together with the breadcrumbs, lemon juice, parsley, oatmeal and suet. Season.

Spoon all but 60 ml (4 level tbsp) stuffing into the chicken. Gently ease the chicken skin away from either side of the breastbone to form two pockets. Press in the reserved stuffing. Heat enough oil to cover the base of a flameproof casserole – there should not be too much space around the chicken. Brown the chicken and take it out.

Put the remaining 225 g (8 oz) onion, the milk and bayleaf into the casserole. Return the chicken and cover. Cook in the oven at 180°C (350°F) mark 4 for about 1¼ hours until tender.

Remove the chicken to a serving dish and keep it warm. Thicken the pan contents with cornflour mixed to a paste with water in the usual way; adjust the seasoning. Serve with carved chicken.

Not suitable for freezing.

Chicken with Cumin and Cider

1 large red skinned eating
   apple
15 ml (1 tbsp) vegetable oil
50 g (2 oz) butter
225 g (½ lb) cooking apples,
   peeled and sliced

4 chicken leg portions
1 small onion, skinned and
   sliced
5 ml (1 level tsp) ground
   cumin
15 ml (1 level tbsp) flour

300 ml (½ pint) jellied chicken
   stock
150 ml (¼ pint) dry cider
salt and freshly ground
   pepper

SERVES 4

Quarter and core the eating apple, halve each quarter lengthwise. Heat the oil and butter in a flameproof casserole and sauté the apple until golden but still crisp. Remove from the fat and reserve. Sauté the chicken joints in the residual fat until golden and take out of the pan. Add the cooking apple and onion, sauté for 3 minutes and stir in the cumin and flour and cook for a further 1 minute. Stir in the stock and cider, season and bring to the boil, replace the chicken.

Cover the pan and simmer gently for 15 minutes. Turn the chicken pieces over. Re-cover the pan and cook for a further 15 minutes, or until the chicken is quite tender.

Garnish the dish with sautéed apple.

Not suitable for freezing.

Moroccan Lemon Chicken

1 lemon
60 ml (4 level tbsp) thick
    honey
2.5 ml (½ level tsp) ground
    white pepper

pinch of saffron
2.5 ml (½ level tsp) mild curry
    powder
pinch of allspice
5 ml (1 level tsp) salt

30 ml (2 tbsp) vegetable oil
8 chicken drumsticks
200 ml (7 fl oz) chicken stock
chopped parsley to garnish

SERVES 4

Halve the lemon lengthwise and cut into thin slices discarding pips.

Mix 30 ml (2 tbsp) honey with the saffron, pepper, curry powder, allspice and salt.
Add the lemon slices, cover and marinate overnight.

Simmer the lemon with the marinade, and 300 ml (½ pint) water in a tightly covered
flameproof casserole for 1 hour, or until really tender.

Melt the oil in a sauté pan, add the remaining honey and drumsticks, fry over a
moderate heat, turning frequently until a rich dark brown.

Add the lemon mixture and stock, bring to the boil, cover and simmer for
15–20 minutes. Adjust the seasoning, adding more honey if necessary. Garnish with
chopped parsley. Serve with rice or couscous (see Vegetable Couscous, page 111, for
preparation), and leaf spinach.

Not suitable for freezing.

Chicken Pot-Roast with Walnuts

1.6 kg (3½ lb) oven-ready
    chicken
25 g (1 oz) butter
15 ml (1 tbsp) vegetable oil
350 g (12 oz) celery, sliced
    and washed
200 g (7 oz) carrots, peeled
    and cut into chunks
200 g (7 oz) leeks, sliced
    and washed

50 g (2 oz) button
    mushrooms, wiped
25 g (1 oz) walnuts

For the stuffing:
knob of butter
½ small onion, skinned and
    finely chopped
25 g (1 oz) mushrooms,
    wiped

30 ml (2 level tbsp) chopped
    walnuts
25 g (1 oz) fresh
    breadcrumbs
5 ml (1 tsp) chopped fresh
    parsley
1 egg, size 6, beaten
salt and freshly ground
    pepper

SERVES 6

For the stuffing, melt the butter and sauté the onion and finely chopped mushrooms
until just soft. Stir in the walnuts, breadcrumbs and parsley with enough beaten egg to
bind. Season to taste. Stuff the neck cavity of the chicken and truss.

Melt the 25 g (1 oz) butter with oil and fry the chicken to brown it on all sides.
Remove and place in a deep ovenproof casserole with a lid.

Sauté the vegetables and walnuts in the remaining fat until lightly browned. Add to
the casserole. Cover and cook in the oven at 150°C (300°F) mark 2 for about 2 hours
until tender.

Not suitable for freezing.

Chicken with Lime and Tarragon

25 g (1 oz) butter
6 chicken breast portions on the bone
1 medium onion, skinned and sliced

45 ml (3 level tbsp) flour
400 ml ($\frac{3}{4}$ pint) chicken stock
2 limes
2.5 ml ($\frac{1}{2}$ level tsp) dried tarragon

salt and freshly ground pepper
60 ml (4 tbsp) double cream

SERVES 6

Heat the butter in a large, shallow, flameproof casserole and fry the chicken breasts until well browned. Don't overcrowd them in the pan – if necessary brown only half at a time. Remove the chicken from the pan, add the onion and fry until golden. Stir in the flour with the stock and bring the liquid to the boil.

Finely grate the zest from the limes straight into the casserole, add the strained lime juice with the tarragon and seasoning, then replace the chicken.

Cover the casserole tightly and cook in the oven at 180°C (350°F) mark 4 for about 45 minutes, or until the chicken is quite tender.

Skim any fat off the surface of the dish and adjust the seasoning. Stir in the cream and warm gently on top of the stove without boiling.

Suitable for freezing. Freeze without cream. Reheat in the usual way and add cream.

Poussin Italienne

4 single poussins
15 ml (1 tbsp) vegetable oil
25 g (1 oz) butter
450 g (1 lb) potatoes, peeled
175 g (6 oz) button onions, skinned
450 ml ($\frac{3}{4}$ pint) chicken stock

125 g (4 oz) button mushrooms, wiped
30 ml (2 level tbsp) tomato purée
5 ml (1 level tsp) dried oregano
45 ml (3 tbsp) dry sherry

salt and freshly ground pepper
50 g (2 oz) cooked ham, shredded
30 ml (2 level tbsp) cornflour

SERVES 4

Brown the poussins in hot oil and butter in large flameproof casserole. Drain.

Cut the potatoes into small fingers, add to the pan with the onions and mushrooms, cook to a golden brown. Replace the poussins side by side.

Mix stock, tomato paste, oregano and sherry together, season well. Pour over the poussins, cover and cook in the oven at 180°C (350°F) mark 4 about 1 hour, or until all ingredients are tender.

Place the birds with vegetables on a serving plate, leaving the juices in the pan. Add the ham to the juices, adjust the seasoning and thicken with blended cornflour. Bring to the boil, stirring. Spoon over the poussins and serve.

Suitable for freezing. Freeze without ham and thickening. Reheat in usual way and continue as above.

Turkey Paupiettes with Cumin

8 thin turkey escalopes or
700 g (1½ lb) turkey fillet
salt and freshly ground
pepper
450 g (1 lb) pork
sausagemeat or sausages
60 ml (4 level tbsp) mango
chutney

50 g (2 oz) salted peanuts,
chopped
30 ml (2 tbsp) vegetable oil
25 g (1 oz) butter
450 g (1 lb) parsnips, peeled
and sliced
450 g (1 lb) medium onions,
skinned and sliced

15 ml (1 level tbsp) ground
cumin
45 ml (3 level tbsp) flour
45 ml (3 level tbsp)
desiccated coconut
400 ml (¾ pint) chicken stock

SERVES 8

Bat out escalopes or fillet between sheets of damp greaseproof paper, into eight thin pieces; season well.

Mix the sausagemeat (or skinned sausages) with 30 ml (2 level tbsp) chutney, the nuts and seasoning. Divide between the escalopes. Roll up and secure with cocktail sticks.

Brown the paupiettes in the hot fat in a shallow flameproof casserole. Drain from fat.

Add the parsnips, onions, cumin, flour and coconut to residual oil, fry for 2–3 minutes.

Stir in the stock, the remaining chutney and seasoning; bring to the boil and replace the paupiettes in a single layer.

Cover the dish and cook in the oven at 150°C (300°F) mark 2 for about 1½ hours, skim before serving.

Not suitable for freezing.

Turkey Pepper Pot

700 g (1½ lb) white turkey
meat
25 g (1 oz) flour
2.5 ml (½ level tsp) ground
ginger
5 ml (1 level tsp) salt
ground pepper
50 g (2 oz) lard

2.5 ml (½ tsp) Tabasco sauce
397-g (14-oz) can tomatoes
125 g (4 oz) mushrooms,
wiped and sliced
15 ml (1 tbsp)
Worcestershire sauce
30 ml (2 level tbsp) soft
brown sugar

30 ml (2 tbsp) wine vinegar
2 small garlic cloves, skinned
and crushed
1 bayleaf
2 medium red peppers, seeded
and sliced

SERVES 4

Cut the flesh into 2.5-cm (1-inch) pieces. Combine the flour with ginger, salt, pepper and coat the cubes well.

Heat the lard in a deep flameproof casserole, then brown the turkey a few pieces at a time.

Return the turkey to the casserole and add the rest of the ingredients except the peppers. Bring to the boil, cover, reduce heat, simmer for 30–35 minutes.

Add the peppers to the casserole and simmer for a further 10 minutes.

Suitable for freezing. Freeze without peppers. Reheat in the usual way and add peppers.

Turkey Sauté with Chilli and Coconut

450 g (1 lb) boneless turkey
thigh meat
25 g (1 oz) butter
1.25 ml (¼ level tsp) chilli
powder

45 ml (3 level tbsp)
desiccated coconut
200 ml (7 fl oz) chicken stock
30 ml (2 level tbsp) mango
chutney

salt and freshly ground
pepper
6 dates – fresh or dried

SERVES 4

Cut meat into 2.5-cm (1-inch) pieces, discarding any skin.

Heat the butter in a flameproof casserole and brown the turkey meat all over.

Sprinkle the chilli powder and coconut into the pan and sauté gently for 1 minute.

Pour in the stock, add the chutney and bring to the boil. Season.

Cover the pan and simmer for about 40 minutes or until the turkey meat is quite tender.

Halve and stone the dates and stir into the pan; warm through gently to serving temperature. Serve with boiled rice.

Not suitable for freezing.

Turkey in Spiced Yogurt

A mild aromatic dish that's not at all hot. The sweetness of coriander balances the slightly bitter cumin and there's just a hint of ginger.

about 1.1 kg (2½ lb) turkey
leg meat on the bone
7.5 ml (1½ level tsp) ground
cumin
7.5 ml (1½ level tsp) ground
coriander
2.5 ml (½ level tsp) ground
turmeric

2.5 ml (½ level tsp) ground
ginger
salt and freshly ground
pepper
300 ml (½ pint) natural
yogurt
30 ml (2 tbsp) lemon juice
225 g (½ lb) onion, skinned

45 ml (3 tbsp) vegetable oil
45 ml (3 level tbsp)
desiccated coconut
30 ml (2 level tbsp) flour
150 ml (¼ pint) chicken stock
or water
snipped parsley to garnish

SERVES 6

Cut the turkey meat off the bone into large fork-sized pieces discarding the skin; there should be about 900 g (2 lb) meat. In a large bowl mix the spices with the seasoning, yogurt and lemon juice. Stir well until evenly blended. Fold through the turkey meat until coated with the yogurt mixture. Cover tightly with cling film and refrigerate for several hours.

Slice the onion and lightly brown in the hot oil in a medium-sized flameproof casserole. Add the coconut and flour and fry gently, stirring for about 1 minute. Off the heat stir in the turkey with its marinade, and the stock. Return to the heat and bring slowly to the boil, stirring all the time. Cover tightly and cook in the oven at 170°C (325°F) mark 3 for 1–1¼ hours, or until the turkey is tender. Adjust the seasoning and serve garnished with parsley.

Not suitable for freezing.

Casseroled Turkey in Red Wine

450–700 g (1–1½ lb) boneless
turkey meat
15 g (½ oz) butter
15 ml (1 tbsp) vegetable oil
125 g (¼ lb) lean streaky
rashers, rinded

30 ml (2 level tbsp) flour
good pinch of dried thyme
bayleaf
150 ml (¼ pint) red wine
salt and freshly ground
pepper

300 ml (½ pint) of water
butter and vegetable oil for
frying
12 small onions or shallots,
skinned
chopped parsley to garnish

SERVES 4

Cut meat into 2.5 cm (1 inch) pieces, discarding any skin. Melt the butter with the oil. When frothing, gradually add turkey meat in a single layer. Brown well. Remove and place in a casserole. Add snipped bacon rashers to the fat and fry until they begin to brown. Add to the turkey.

Stir flour, thyme, bayleaf into the pan fat and cook gently for a few minutes. Slowly stir in red wine and water. Bring to the boil, stirring. Season and pour over the turkey.

Cover the casserole tightly, cook in the oven at 150°C (300°F) mark 2 for about 2 hours.

Half an hour before the end of the cooking time, melt a little butter with oil in a frying pan. Brown the onions slowly. When tender, add to the casserole. Garnish before serving.

Suitable for freezing. Freeze without onions and garnish. Reheat in the usual way and add garnish.

Turkey Ragout

700 g (1½ lb) boneless dark
turkey meat
1 medium onion, skinned
225 g (8 oz) cooking apple,
peeled
350 g (12 oz) carrot, peeled

30 ml (2 tbsp) vegetable oil
salt and freshly ground
pepper
10 ml (2 level tsp) ground
paprika
30 ml (2 level tbsp) flour

10 ml (2 level tsp) ground
coriander
2.5 ml (½ level tsp) ground
turmeric
400 ml (¾ pint) chicken stock

SERVES 4

Cut up the meat into fork-size pieces discarding the skin. Slice the onion, apple and carrot. Brown the turkey all over in hot oil and remove from the pan.

Add the onion, apple and carrots to the pan with the seasoning, spices and flour and fry for 2–3 minutes, stirring.

Blend in the stock and bring to the boil, replace the turkey meat. Cover the pan and *simmer* for about 1 hour.

Adjust seasoning and serve.

Suitable for freezing. Reheat in the usual way.

Duckling Ratatouille

1.8 kg (4 lb) oven ready
  duckling
225 g (8 oz) aubergines
225 g (8 oz) courgettes
salt and freshly ground
  pepper

1 medium onion, skinned
15 ml (1 tbsp) vegetable oil
25 g (1 oz) butter
flour
2.5 ml (½ level tsp) dried sage
150 ml (¼ pint) dry red wine

150 ml (¼ pint) chicken stock
225 g (8 oz) tomatoes,
  skinned
50 g (2 oz) fresh white
  breadcrumbs

SERVES 4

Joint the duckling into eight pieces discarding the back bone. Remove all skin and fat, reserving 50 g (2 oz) fat. Cut this into fine strips.

Wipe the aubergines and courgettes and cut into 0.5-cm (¼-inch) slices, sprinkle with salt and leave to stand for 20 minutes. Pat dry with kitchen paper.

Thinly slice the onions, brown in hot oil and butter in a frying pan. Drain from fat and place in bottom of a 2.3-litre (4-pint) ovenproof casserole. Toss the duckling in flour and brown on both sides in the frying pan. Place on top of the onions.

Layer up the dish with aubergines, courgettes, seasoning, sage, red wine and stock. Top with the sliced tomatoes, breadcrumbs and duck fat.

Cover and bake in the oven at 200°C (400°F) mark 6 for about 1¼ hours.

Suitable for freezing. Reheat in the usual way.

Marinated Duckling Casserole

two 2-kg (4½-lb) oven ready
  ducklings
2 large juicy oranges
45 ml (3 tbsp) brandy

salt and freshly ground
  pepper
50 g (2 oz) butter or
  margarine

2 bayleaves
700 g (1½ lb) swedes, peeled
45 ml (3 level tbsp) flour
snipped parsley to garnish

SERVES 8

The day before slice the duckling flesh off the bone reserving skin. Cut the meat into finger sized pieces and place in a shallow dish. Grate over the orange rind, strain over the juice and stir in the brandy, bayleaves and seasoning. Cover and marinate in a cool place overnight.

Prepare 300 ml (½ pint) strong stock from the bones and giblets. Strain the marinade off the duckling and reserve, but discard the bayleaves. Brown the duckling well in hot fat in a flameproof casserole, then lift them from the fat.

Cut the swede into fat matchsticks and brown in residual fat.

Stir in the flour followed by the stock and marinade. Bring to the boil, season and replace the duckling.

Cover the casserole and cook in the oven at 180°C (350°F) mark 4 for about 1¼ hours or until tender. Place the duckling skin cut into thin strips in a baking dish in the oven.

To serve, adjust seasoning. Garnish with duckling skin and plenty of snipped parsley.

Not suitable for freezing.

Sauté of Duckling with Peas

4 duckling joints, about
  350 g (12 oz) each
15 ml (1 level tbsp) flour
300 ml (½ pint) chicken stock

150 ml (¼ pint) red wine
15 ml (1 tbsp) chopped fresh
  sage or 5 ml (1 level tsp)
  dried

salt and freshly ground
  pepper
450 g (1 lb) fresh peas,
  podded

SERVES 4

Ease the skin and fat off the duckling joints, halve the leg joint. Snip the skin into small pieces. Brown these in a large flameproof casserole until crisp, and reserve.

Drain off all but 45 ml (3 tbsp) fat from the pan and brown the duckling joints.

Sprinkle in the flour, stir to combine with fat and cook gently for 1 minute. Pour in the stock, wine, sage and seasoning and bring to the boil. Cover the pan and simmer for 25 minutes, then turn the duckling pieces over. Add the peas to the pan, submerging them as far as possible. Cover and continue simmering for about 25 minutes until the duckling and peas are tender.

Adjust seasoning and garnish with crispy duck skin.

Not suitable for freezing.

Brandied Duckling with Orange

If you're lucky enough to pick fresh sage, then use about six leaves finely chopped. Flambéing with brandy takes up any greasiness.

two 1.8 kg (4 lb) oven ready
  ducklings
2 large oranges
60 ml (4 level tbsp) flour

2.5 ml (½ level tsp) dried sage
salt and freshly ground
  pepper
50 g (2 oz) butter

350 g (12 oz) celery, wiped
  and sliced
60 ml (4 tbsp) brandy
300 ml (½ pint) chicken stock

SERVES 6

Using game or sharp kitchen scissors split the ducklings in half along the breast bone. Cut out and discard the backbone and divide each side of the duckling into three – a leg joint, wing joint with a portion of breast attached, and breast joint. Pull off the skin, discard all the fat and trim off the wing pinions and 'knobbly' leg ends.

Finely grate the rind off the oranges and mix with the flour, sage and some seasoning. Coat the duckling joints in the flour mixture and brown, a few at a time, in the hot butter in a large flameproof casserole. Remove from the pan. To pan juices add the celery with any remaining flour, cook for 2–3 minutes, stirring.

Replace the duckling, mixing it with the celery and flame with the brandy. Pour in the stock with 120 ml (8 tbsp) strained orange juice and bring to the boil. Cover tightly and cook in the oven at 180°C (350°F) mark 4 for about 1¼ hours, or until tender – turn the duckling at half time.

Place the duckling in an oval edged dish, boil up the juices, adjust seasoning and spoon over the duckling.

Suitable for freezing. Reheat in the usual way.

Game

Though most people would agree that a tender young game bird is at its best roasted, there are always occasions when either a change is required, or the bird is neither young nor tender. A casserole of any game bird or animal, especially with the addition of wine, beer, port or brandy, offers a meal fit for a king – which indeed it has done for centuries.

Hanging Game

If you live in the country you are likely to be able to obtain freshly killed birds and animals. These should be hung for a few days in a cool, dry place for the flesh to be tender and well-flavoured. The length of hanging depends on personal taste and on weather conditions – anything from two or three days for a mildly gamey flavour, to up to 10 days for those who like their game quite 'high'. As you will probably be unable to ascertain the age of ready prepared birds, it is probably safest to casserole them, as only young and tender birds are successfully roasted. Rabbit, hare and venison are all delicious casseroled – as with all game, the meat benefits from not being allowed to dry out.

Many game birds are quite small, and though you can casserole two or more birds at a time, the extra vegetables and sauce makes the meal go much further. As most game casseroles are quite rich, a tasty fresh green salad, or orange salad is always a good accompaniment.

Cider Baked Rabbit with Cabbage

1.4 kg (3 lb) firm white cabbage
225 g (½ lb) streaky bacon rashers, rinded
2 medium onions, skinned and sliced
60 ml (4 tbsp) vegetable oil

350 g (12 oz) cooking apple, peeled and sliced
salt and freshly ground pepper
8 rabbit joints, about 1.4 kg (3 lb) total weight
60 ml (4 level tbsp) flour

15 ml (3 level tsp) French mustard
300 ml (½ pint) dry cider
450 ml (¾ pint) chicken stock
chopped parsley to garnish

SERVES 8

Coarsely shred the cabbage, wash and drain. Snip the bacon into small pieces.

Heat the oil in a large frying pan and lightly brown the bacon, onion and apple. Lift out of the pan with draining spoons, mix with the cabbage and plenty of seasoning and place in a large ovenproof casserole. Brown the rabbit joints well in the reheated residual oil and place on top of the cabbage.

Stir the flour and mustard into the pan. Gradually add the cider and stock, stirring. Season and bring to the boil.

Pour over the rabbit; cover tightly and cook in the oven at 170°C (325°F) mark 3 for 1½–1¾ hours, or until the rabbit is tender. Adjust the seasoning. Garnish with plenty of parsley.

Not suitable for freezing.

Rabbit Casserole with Sage Dumplings

Plentiful supplies of wild rabbit used to make a change from pork for country families, and even today rabbit is good value for money.

125 g (4 oz) streaky bacon	1 bayleaf	600 ml (1 pint) stock
4 rabbit joints	225 g (8 oz) carrots, peeled	75 g (3 oz) self-raising flour
4 sticks celery, trimmed and	and sliced	40 g (1½ oz) shredded suet
chopped	30 ml (2 level tbsp) flour	5 ml (1 tsp) chopped fresh
2 leeks, trimmed, sliced and	salt and freshly ground	sage leaves
washed	pepper	

SERVES 4

Rind and snip the bacon into a flameproof casserole. Fry until the fat runs. Add the rabbit and fry gently, add celery, leeks, bayleaf and carrots. Sprinkle in the plain flour and stir well. Now add the stock a little at a time and bring to the boil, stirring. Season to taste. Cover the casserole and cook in the oven at 170°C (325°F) mark 3 for about 1½ hours or until rabbit is tender. Combine the self-raising flour, suet, sage and seasoning. Mix to a soft dough with cold water. Divide the dumpling dough into four portions then shape evenly into balls and place on top of casserole. Cover again and cook for 20–25 minutes until dumplings are well risen and cooked through.

Suitable for freezing. Freeze without dumplings. Reheat in the usual way, add dumplings and continue as above.

Jugged Hare

1 hare, jointed – about 1.6 kg	50 g (2 oz) butter	2 medium onions, skinned
(3½ lb) with its blood	900 ml (1½ pint) beef stock	12 cloves
75 ml (5 level tbsp) seasoned	150 ml (¼ pint) port	salt and freshly ground
flour	5 ml (1 level tsp) dried	pepper
125 g (4 oz) rindless streaky	marjoram	snipped parsley to garnish
bacon	45 ml (3 level tbsp)	
5 ml (1 tsp) vinegar	redcurrant jelly	

SERVES 6

Wipe the hare and divide into smaller pieces if necessary. Toss in the seasoned flour. Snip the bacon into small pieces. Mix the blood with vinegar, cover and refrigerate.

Brown the bacon in its own fat in a large flameproof casserole and take out of the pan. Add the butter to the pan and lightly brown the hare portions. Add the stock, port, herbs and redcurrant jelly with the onions studded with the cloves. Replace the bacon and season well. Bring to the boil, cover and cook in the oven at 170°C (325°F) mark 3 for about 3 hours, or until the hare is tender. Take the hare out of its juices, place in a deep serving dish, cover and keep warm. Discard the onions.

Mix the blood with some cooking juices until smooth. Add to the pan and heat through without boiling, adjust seasoning, pour over hare and garnish with parsley.

Suitable for freezing. Reheat in the usual way.

Salmis of Pheasant

Salmis, a richly-flavoured ragout of game, should never be made with leftovers. The jointed bird is freshly roasted until almost done then cooked in a wine sauce. Partridges and Guinea fowl may also be cooked in the same way.

a brace of pheasants	300 ml (½ pint) chicken stock	125 g (4 oz) celery, diced
butter	bayleaf	45 ml (3 level tbsp) flour
salt and freshly ground pepper	225 g (8 oz) carrots, peeled and diced	60 ml (4 tbsp) port or reduced red wine
slices of carrot and onion for flavouring	1 medium onion, skinned and roughly chopped	fried croûtons to garnish

SERVES 4–6

Wash and dry the pheasants. Place a small knob of butter inside each bird and spread 25 g (1 oz) butter over the breasts; season well. Place the birds in a small roasting tin and pour the chicken stock around. Roast in the oven at 200°C (400°F) mark 6 for 40 minutes basting occasionally.

Lift the birds out on to a large chopping board. Pour off the pan juices and reserve. Slice through the flesh running along the breast of the bird until the bone is reached. Using strong kitchen or game scissors snip right through the breast bone to open out the bird. Cut through the skin around the legs then push the joints away from the carcass until completely detached. Snip firmly down either side of the backbone to remove it; reserve the bone. Divide each breast portion into two, snipping through the bone. Place the joints on a plate, cover loosely and store in a cool place.

Place the backbones in a small saucepan. Pour over the reserved roasting juices. Add the flavouring vegetables with the bayleaf and seasoning and sufficient water to just cover the bones. Bring slowly to the boil, simmer uncovered for about 30 minutes, or until about 400 ml (¾ pint) stock remains. Strain off and reserve.

Melt 50 g (2 oz) butter or margarine in a medium-sized flameproof casserole. Add the carrots, onion and celery, cover the pan and cook over a moderate heat for about 10 minutes until the vegetables soften and tinge with colour. Add flour, cook for 1 minute, stirring. Blend in 400 ml (¾ pint) stock and port. Season, bring to the boil, take off heat. Put the pheasant joints into the casserole pushing them down among the vegetables. The legs take longer to cook so put these in first. Baste any exposed pheasant flesh with sauce. Return slowly to the boil, then cover tightly, placing a piece of greaseproof paper under the lid. Cook in the oven at 170°C (325°F) mark 3 for about 1¼ hours. Test the leg joints with a fine skewer; when cooked the juices should run clear and the meat ease readily away from the bone. The flesh on older pheasants could well take longer to tenderise. Garnish with fried croûtons.

Not suitable for freezing.

Old English Game Stew

Rich, meaty and delicious, with the chuck steak taking on the pheasant flavour. Even better when made a day ahead.

450 g (1 lb) chuck steak	2 medium onions, skinned	salt and freshly ground
1 large old pheasant	and finely sliced	pepper
50 g (2 oz) butter	45 ml (3 level tbsp) flour	forcemeat balls (see
4 large sticks celery, washed	150 ml (¼ pint) port	page 123)
and coarsely chopped	400 ml (¾ pint) chicken stock	snipped parsley to garnish

SERVES 6

Cut up the steak into strips 5 cm (2 inch) long by 1 cm (2 inch) wide, discarding excess fat. Joint the pheasant into six pieces removing the end wing joints, backbone and any feathers still attached to the skin. Brown the steak pieces in the hot fat in a large flameproof casserole. Remove from the fat, drain, then brown the pheasant joints; remove from the pan. Add the celery and onion to the pan and lightly brown. Stir in the flour, port, stock and seasoning and bring to the boil. Replace the meat and pheasant, cover tightly and cook in the oven at 180°C (350°F) mark 4 for 1½–2 hours, or until the meats are almost tender. Meanwhile, prepare the forcemeat balls. Place them between the meat in the casserole, cover again and return to the oven at 190°C (375°F) mark 5 for a further 30 minutes. Adjust the seasoning and snip parsley over the surface.

Suitable for freezing. Freeze without forcemeat balls. Reheat in the usual way. Add forcemeat balls and continue as above.

Pheasant Casserole with Port and Orange

a brace of young pheasants	finely grated rind and juice of	salt and freshly ground
30 ml (2 tbsp) vegetable oil	2 oranges	pepper
300 ml (½ pint) chicken stock	50 g (2 oz) sultanas	25 g (1 oz) flaked almonds,
120 ml (8 tbsp) port	20 ml (4 level tsp) cornflour	toasted

SERVES 4–6

Wipe the pheasants and brown all over in the hot oil in a large flameproof casserole.

Pour the stock and port over the birds. Add the orange rind and juice with the sultanas and season well. Bring to the boil. Cover tightly and cook in the oven at 170°C (325°F) mark 3 for 1–1½ hours, or until the liquid runs clear when the birds are pierced with a skewer.

Joint each pheasant into 2 or 3 pieces depending on size and arrange them on a serving dish; keep warm.

Boil up the juices with cornflour mixed to a smooth paste with a little water, stirring. Adjust the seasoning and spoon over pheasant. Garnish with flaked almonds.

Suitable for freezing. Freeze without thickening and garnish. Reheat in the usual way. Thicken and garnish.

Poacher's Pie

225 g (8 oz) shortcrust
   pastry (see page 117)
4 rabbit joints, chopped
3–4 rashers bacon, rinded
   and chopped
2 potatoes, peeled and sliced

1 leek, trimmed, washed and
   sliced
salt and freshly ground
   pepper
15 ml (1 tbsp) chopped fresh
   parsley

1.25 ml ($\frac{1}{4}$ level tsp) mixed
   dried herbs
stock or water
beaten egg to glaze

SERVES 4

Make the pastry. Wash the rabbit pieces. Fill a pie dish with alternate layers of rabbit, bacon and vegetables, sprinkling each layer with seasoning and herbs. Half-fill the dish with stock or water, cover with the pastry and make a hole in the centre to let the steam escape. Decorate with leaves made from the pastry trimmings and brush with egg.

Bake in the oven at 220°C (425°F) mark 7 until the pastry is set, then reduce the temperature to 170°C (325°F) mark 3 and cook for about 1¼ hours, until the meat is tender. Cover with foil if the pie starts to become brown.

Not suitable for freezing.

Rich Venison Casserole

1 kg (2 lb) stewing venison
150 ml ($\frac{1}{4}$ pint) red wine
100 ml (4 fl oz) vegetable oil
12 juniper berries, lightly
   crushed
4 cloves
8 black peppercorns

1 garlic clove, skinned and
   crushed
25 g (4 oz) streaky bacon
   rashers, rinded
225 g (8 oz) onions, skinned
   and sliced
30 ml (2 level tbsp) flour

150 ml ($\frac{1}{4}$ pint) beef stock
30 ml (2 tbsp) redcurrant
   jelly
salt and freshly ground
   pepper
chopped parsley to garnish

SERVES 4

Cut the meat into cubes, discarding any fat or gristle. Place in a bowl. Add the wine, half the oil, juniper berries, cloves, peppercorns and garlic. Stir well and leave to marinate for at least 24 hours, stirring occasionally.

Stretch each bacon rasher using a knife, cut in half and roll up. Heat the remaining oil in a flameproof casserole and fry the bacon for about 3 minutes until coloured. Remove from the casserole. Strain the venison from the marinade and quickly fry the meat pieces in several batches until coloured. Add the onions and cook for 3 minutes. Then add the flour and cook for 2 minutes, stirring. Add the stock, redcurrant jelly and the marinade, and replace the meat. Season. Place the bacon rolls on the top of the casserole and bring to the boil.

Cover and cook in the oven at 170°C (325°F) mark 3 for 3 hours until the venison is tender. Garnish with chopped parsley. Serve with extra redcurrant jelly, braised cabbage and creamed potatoes.

Suitable for freezing. Reheat in the usual way.

Casseroled Pigeon in Port Wine

8 pigeons
slices of carrot and onion,
    peppercorns and bayleaves
    for flavouring
50 g (2 oz) butter or
    margarine

450 g (1 lb) onions, skinned
    and diced
450 g (1 lb) swede, peeled
    and diced
350 g (12 oz) celery, wiped
    and diced

45 ml (3 level tbsp) flour
60 ml (4 tbsp) port
salt and freshly ground
    pepper
parsley sprigs or celery leaves
    to garnish

SERVES 8

Remove the breasts from the pigeons, skin and slice into fork-sized pieces. Place carcasses, flavouring vegetables, bayleaves and peppercorns with 1.1 litre (2 pints) water in a large saucepan.

Simmer for about 1 hour or until reduced to 600 ml (1 pint).

Heat the butter in a large pan and quickly brown the pigeon pieces, a few at a time. Remove them from the pan and add the diced vegetables. Cover the pan, reduce heat and cook for about 5 minutes, or until beginning to soften.

Stirring well, toss in the flour and cook for 2 minutes. Add port with 400 ml ($\frac{3}{4}$ pint) stock and bring to the boil. Season well. Stir in the pigeon pieces.

Place in a large ovenproof casserole. Cover and cook in the oven at 150°C (300°F) mark 2 for about 3 hours. Garnish.

Not suitable for freezing.

Wood Pigeons in Beer

4 small wood pigeons
30 ml (2 tbsp) vegetable oil
25 g (1 oz) butter
450 g (1 lb) onions, skinned
    and sliced
45 ml (3 level tbsp) flour

20 ml (4 level tsp) French
    mustard
600 ml (1 pint) light ale
20 ml (4 level tsp) soft brown
    sugar
30 ml (2 tbsp) vinegar

salt and freshly ground
    pepper
142 ml (5 fl oz) soured cream
200-g (7-oz) can of
    pimientos, drained

SERVES 4

Cut the backbone from each pigeon, leaving the rest of the bird whole.

Heat the oil in a large flameproof casserole. Add butter and when frothing, brown the birds lightly on all sides. Remove the birds.

Fry the onions until golden. Stir in the flour, mustard, ale, sugar, vinegar, salt and pepper. Bring to the boil, stirring.

Return the birds to the casserole. Cover tightly and cook in the oven at 170°C (325°F) mark 3 for about 2$\frac{1}{2}$ hours, or until tender.

Serve the pigeon on a heated dish. Reheat the juices with cream and thin sliced pimiento. Spoon over the pigeons.

Suitable for freezing. Freeze without soured cream and pimiento. Reheat in the usual way and add soured cream and pimiento.

Partridge with Grapes

2 young partridges
30 ml (2 tbsp) vegetable oil
175 ml (6 fl oz) chicken stock
90 ml (6 tbsp) dry white
   wine

salt and freshly ground white
   pepper
15 ml (1 level tbsp) cornflour
1 egg yolk
30 ml (2 tbsp) double cream

125 g (4 oz) white grapes,
   skinned, halved, pipped
chopped parsley to garnish

SERVES 2

Halve the partridges and remove the backbones. Carefully pull off the skin.

Heat the oil in a large flameproof casserole and lightly brown the birds on both sides.

Pour over stock and wine, season and bring to the boil. Cover tightly and cook gently on top of the stove for about 25 minutes or until the meat is tender.

Drain the partridges and keep warm on a serving dish. Blend together cornflour, egg yolk and cream. Add to the pan juices with grapes and cook gently without boiling, until the sauce thickens. Adjust the seasoning.

Spoon the sauce over partridges and garnish.

Suitable for freezing. Freeze without cornflour, egg and cream. Reheat in the usual way and thicken as above.

Casseroled Grouse with Brandy

2 old grouse
125 g (4 oz) rindless streaky
   bacon — thick rasher
30 ml (2 tbsp) vegetable oil

60 ml (4 tbsp) brandy
225 g ($\frac{1}{2}$ lb) cooking apples,
   peeled, cored and chopped
400 ml ($\frac{3}{4}$ pint) chicken stock

salt and freshly ground
   pepper
15 ml (1 level tbsp) cornflour
chopped parsley to garnish

SERVES 4

Halve the grouse and cut away the backbone, then wash and dry them.

Cut the bacon into small pieces and lightly brown with the grouse in hot oil in a flameproof casserole.

Add the brandy, heat gently, ignite and allow to burn until the flames subside.

Add the apples to the grouse with boiling stock and seasoning. Cover tightly; cook in the oven at 170°C (325°F) mark 3 for about 2½ hours, or until the birds are tender.

Lift the grouse on to a warm serving dish. Boil up the juices and thicken with cornflour in the usual way. Spoon over the grouse and garnish.

Suitable for freezing. Freeze without thickening. Reheat in the usual way, and thicken as above.

Fish in White Wine (see page 100)

Creamed Quail Casserole

4 quail
seasoned flour
100 g (4 oz) button
   mushrooms, wiped

50 g (2 oz) butter
60 ml (4 tbsp) dry sherry
salt and freshly ground
   pepper

142 ml (5 fl oz) soured cream
chopped parsley to garnish

SERVES 4

Coat the quail in the seasoned flour. Melt the butter in a flameproof casserole and brown the birds evenly. Add the mushrooms and sauté them, then add the sherry and seasoning. Cover and cook in the oven at 190°C (375°F) mark 5 for 40 minutes. Stir in the soured cream, adjust the seasoning and serve sprinkled with chopped parsley.

Not suitable for freezing.

Pigeon with Prunes

4 young pigeons
50 g (2 oz) lard or dripping
1 rasher fat bacon
1 medium onion, skinned and
   chopped
2 carrots, skinned and
   chopped

225 g (8 oz) tomatoes,
   chopped
50 g (2 oz) mushrooms, wiped
600 ml (1 pint) beef stock
1 bayleaf
1 bouquet garni
pinch of sugar

salt and freshly ground
   pepper
225 ml (8 fl oz) red wine
12 prunes
sweet chutney
12 almonds, blanched

SERVES 4

Brown the flour-dusted pigeons whole in dripping. Remove and place in a deep casserole. Add the bacon and chopped vegetables to the dripping and brown. Add the stock and herbs, and simmer for 10 minutes. Push through a sieve, adjust seasoning and add 100 ml (4 fl oz) wine. Pour over birds and simmer in a closed casserole for $1\frac{1}{2}$–2 hours. Meanwhile, simmer the prunes in the rest of the wine until tender, remove their stones, fill with chutney and one almond. Remove the birds into open dish and pour over sauce. Garnish with prunes and parsley.

Not suitable for freezing.

Vegetable Couscous (see page 111) with Boston Beans (see page 113)

Fish & Seafood

Many Mediterranean countries, Scandinavia and the east coast of the United States produce the most delectable fish stews. It is therefore extraordinary that these islands, surrounded as they are by some of the best fishing waters, teeming with such a variety of fish, that we have not evolved a national fish stew, and should be so unadventurous in producing this sort of substantial fish dish.

Though no fish really needs the long, slow cooking that many cuts of meat require, casseroling has several advantages over the more conventional methods of frying, grilling or poaching fish. For one thing, cooking fish slowly in the oven prevents fishy smells from pervading the house – a distinct hazard if you are offering dinner guests a fish dish, and these recipes are certainly good enough for that. Fish is often apt to fall apart when transferred to a serving dish. If baked in a casserole it will retain its shape until it reaches the plate. The success of a fish dish more often than not depends on its accompanying sauce, and when it is casseroled the herbs, spices, wine, cider or vegetables have more time and opportunity to penetrate the often bland fish. Cheap fish like coley or frozen packets of cod, haddock or whiting which are usually destined to undergo dreary deep frying can be gently simmered on a bed of herbs or vegetables surrounded by wine or cider making wonderful sauces which can be later thickened and enriched with cream or eggs.

Generally speaking, no fish needs more than about half an hour's cooking. Octopus, squid and eel take longer while most shellfish need very little indeed, though no harm is done in simmering gently while other ingredients cook through.

Fish in White Wine

1.1 kg (2½ lb) cod, haddock
  or other white fish
  fillet
450 g (1 lb) courgettes, wiped
  and sliced thinly
350 g (12 oz) onion, skinned
  and sliced

50 g (2 oz) butter
30 ml (2 level tbsp) flour
15 ml (1 level tbsp) paprika
300 ml (½ pint) dry white
  wine
397-g (14-oz) can tomatoes
5 ml (1 level tsp) dried basil

1 garlic clove, skinned and
  crushed
salt and freshly ground
  pepper
190-g (6¾-oz) can pimiento,
  drained
fried croûtons

SERVES 8 ———————————————————————— *Illustrated in colour opposite page 96*

Skin the fish and cut into 5-cm (2-inch) pieces.

Melt the butter in a large frying pan, add the courgettes, onion, flour and paprika and fry gently for 3–4 minutes, stirring occasionally.

Stir in the wine, the contents of can of tomatoes, basil, garlic and seasoning. Bring to the boil.

In a large ovenproof dish layer up the fish, sliced pimiento and sauce mixture, seasoning well.

Cover the dish tightly and cook in the oven at 170°C (325°F) mark 3 for 50–60 minutes, adjust seasoning. Garnish with croûtes of French bread.

Not suitable for freezing.

Summer Fish Hot Pot

700 g (1½ lb) firm white fish
  fillets (cod, haddock or
  monkfish)
275 g (10 oz) fresh fennel,
  untrimmed weight
40 g (1½ oz) butter

50 g (2 oz) flour
450 ml (¾ pint) chicken stock
salt and freshly ground
  pepper
60 ml (4 tbsp) chopped, fresh
  parsley

10 ml (2 tsp) lemon juice
450 g (1 lb) new potatoes,
  boiled
parsley to garnish

SERVES 4 ————————————————————————

Skin the fish and place in a pan of shallow water. Bring to the boil, remove from the heat and drain. Cut into fork-size pieces.

Trim the fennel and cut into thin slices, blanch in boiling salted water for 2 minutes. Drain.

In a flameproof casserole, make a roux using the butter and flour. Cook for 2 minutes then gradually add the stock. Bring to the boil, and cook for 2 minutes. Season.

Add the fennel, parsley and lemon juice to the sauce and mix well. Stir in the fish taking care not to break up the flesh; allow to cool.

Slice the cooked potatoes, stir the ends into the casserole. Arrange the slices of potato on top and cover the dish with buttered foil.

Bake covered in the oven at 180°C (350°F) mark 4 for about 50 minutes or until the fish is cooked. Garnish with chopped parsley.

Not suitable for freezing.

Chunky Fish Casserole

Italy is renowned for its fish dishes and varieties of *cassola* or *buridda* (fish casserole) are found across the country. Nearly every region has access to the sea and there are plenty of fish from the freshwater lakes too. It is best to serve the casserole, with its delicious juices, in soup plates, with plenty of crusty bread.

125 g (4 oz) small pasta
   shells
450 g (1 lb) fillets of sole,
   skinned
6 scallops
60 ml (4 level tbsp) flour
salt and freshly ground
   pepper
200-g (7-oz) can whole
   artichoke hearts

75 g (3 oz) butter
1 green pepper, seeded and
   chopped
1 yellow pepper, seeded and
   chopped
175 g (6 oz) onion, skinned
   and sliced
225 g (½ lb) button
   mushrooms, wiped and
   sliced

1 garlic clove, skinned and
   crushed
300 ml (½ pint) dry vermouth
150 ml (¼ pint) chicken stock
5 ml (1 level tsp) dried sage
   or 15 ml (1 level tbsp)
   fresh chopped
225 g (½ lb) peeled prawns
crusty bread to accompany

SERVES 6

Cook the pasta shells in boiling salted water for three-quarters of the time recommended on the packet. Drain in a colander and run cold water over the pasta. Cut the sole into finger-sized strips. Ease the black thread and any membrane away from the scallops, cut the flesh into chunks. Toss the prepared fish in the flour, seasoned with salt and milled pepper. Quarter the artichoke hearts. Melt 50 g (2 oz) of the butter in a large frying pan. Add the peppers, onions and mushrooms and fry over a high heat for a few minutes. Remove from the pan using draining spoons and place in a deep 2.8-litre (5 pint) ovenproof dish. Add the remaining butter to the pan and when frothing add the sole and scallops with the garlic. Fry for a couple of minutes, turning gently to avoid breaking up the fish. Stir in the vermouth, stock, sage and seasoning and bring up to the boil. Pour over the vegetables. Add the artichoke hearts, prawns and pasta shells and stir gently to mix the ingredients. Cover the dish and bake in the oven at 180°C (350°F) mark 4 for about 40 minutes. Adjust seasoning and serve hot.

Not suitable for freezing.

Algarve Fish Stew

450 g (1 lb) dogfish or other
  firm white fish
225 g (8 oz) sardines or
  sprats
1 litre (1¾ pints) mussels or
  about 450 g (1 lb) weight
30 ml (2 tbsp) vegetable oil

2 medium onions, skinned
  and sliced
1 green pepper, seeded and
  sliced
450 g (1 lb) fresh tomatoes,
  skinned and chopped
5 ml (1 tsp) Tabasco sauce

bayleaf
salt and freshly ground
  pepper
300 ml (½ pint) white wine
4 slices bread, crusts removed
butter for spreading

SERVES 4

Skin the dogfish and cut into chunks. Clean the sardines, remove the heads and tails and cut into chunks. Scrub the mussels, discarding any which are open. Place in a pan, cover and cook over a high heat for about 8 minutes or until the mussels have opened. Remove all but four from their shells.

In a frying pan heat the oil and cook the onions and pepper for about 5 minutes, until starting to soften, then add the tomatoes and cook for a further 5 minutes and then add the Tabasco.

Layer up the fish and vegetables in a deep casserole dish and add the bayleaf and seasoning. Pour over the wine. Push the four mussels in shells into the top layer. Butter the bread and cut into triangles. Lay on top of the casserole and cover. Cook in the oven at 180°C (350°F) mark 4 for 45 minutes. Uncover the casserole and allow the croûtes to crisp for about a further 10 minutes.

Not suitable for freezing.

Spicy Fish Pilau

25 g (1 oz) butter
175 g (6 oz) onion, skinned
  and sliced
1 garlic clove, skinned and
  crushed
225 g (8 oz) long-grain rice
5 ml (1 level tsp) turmeric
2.5 ml (½ level tsp) ground
  coriander

2.5 ml (½ level tsp) ground
  cumin
freshly ground pepper
350 g (12 oz) tomatoes,
  skinned and roughly
  chopped
450 g (1 lb) coley fillet or
  monkfish, skinned and
  cubed

5 ml (1 level tsp) salt
10 ml (2 level tsp) chopped
  fresh mint or 2.5 ml
  (½ level tsp) dried
300 ml (½ pint) chicken stock
fresh mint or parsley sprigs
  to garnish

SERVES 4

Melt the butter in a saucepan and fry the onion for 5 minutes.

Stir in the garlic and rice and fry until transparent. Add spices, salt, pepper and tomatoes and cook for 1 minute.

Cut the fish into 2.5-cm (1-inch) strips and combine with the mint. Spread some of the rice on to the base of a 600-ml (1-pint) ovenproof casserole. Cover with a tight-fitting lid. Alternate with layers of fish and rice, ending with a layer of rice.

Pour over the stock, cover tightly and cook in the oven at 180°C (350°F) mark 4 for about 45 minutes. Stir it through and serve garnished.

Not suitable for freezing.

Trout Braised in White Wine

4 small trout, with heads on
salt and freshly ground
   pepper
1 large onion, skinned and
   sliced

50 g (2 oz) butter
2 stalks celery, trimmed and
   sliced
2 carrots, peeled and very
   thinly sliced

300 ml (½ pint) white wine
bouquet garni
15 ml (1 level tbsp) flour

SERVES 4

Clean and dry the trout and season the insides with salt and pepper. Heat half the butter in a small pan, add the vegetables and stir well to cover with butter. Cover and 'sweat' for 5 minutes. Lay the vegetables in a greased ovenproof casserole and lay the fish on top. Pour over the wine and add the bouquet garni. Cover tightly and cook in the oven at 180°C (350°F) mark 4 for about 25 minutes until the trout are cooked.

Lift the trout and vegetables on to a serving dish, and keep warm. Pour the cooking liquor into a small pan. Blend together the remaining butter and flour and whisk into the sauce and simmer gently until thickened. Pour over the trout and serve hot.

Not suitable for freezing.

Curried Fish

450 g (1 lb) monkfish, hake
   or coley
1 garlic clove, skinned and
   crushed
2.5 cm (½ inch) piece of fresh
   ginger

2.5 ml (½ level tsp) chilli
   powder
5 ml (1 level tsp) garam
   masala
150 ml (¼ pint) natural
   yogurt

2.5 ml (½ level tsp) turmeric
50 ml (2 tbsp) vegetable oil
1 large onion, skinned and
   sliced
50 g (2 oz) creamed coconut

SERVES 4

Skin the fish if necessary, cut into chunks and place in a bowl. Add the garlic. Peel the ginger and chop very finely, and add to the fish. Add the turmeric, chilli powder and garam masala to the yogurt and pour over the fish. Stir gently to coat the fish and leave in a cool place to marinate for at least 30 minutes.

Heat the oil in a flameproof casserole and cook the onion for about 10 minutes until very soft. Strain the fish from the marinade and sauté the pieces in the fat for a few minutes. Gradually add the marinade and coconut stirring all the time. Cover and cook over a very gentle heat for about 25 minutes until the fish is tender.

Not suitable for freezing.

Prawns Creole

750 g (1½ lb) uncooked large
  prawns
50 g (2 oz) butter or block
  margarine
1 large onion, skinned and
  chopped

30 ml (2 level tbsp) flour
2 red peppers, seeded and
  sliced
4 stalks celery, trimmed and
  sliced
300 ml (½ pint) white wine

1.25 ml (¼ level tsp) chilli
  powder
450 g (1 lb) fresh tomatoes,
  skinned and quartered
salt and freshly ground
  pepper

SERVES 4

Remove the shells from the prawns, and rinse them well under cold water. Pat dry with kitchen paper and toss in the flour.

Heat the fat in a flameproof casserole and fry the prawns until golden. Remove from the casserole. Add the onion, peppers and celery and cook for about 5 minutes until starting to colour. Add the chilli powder, tomatoes, wine and seasoning, and replace the prawns. Stir well and bring to the boil. Cover and simmer for about 30 minutes until the prawns are tender. Check the seasoning and serve with boiled rice.

Not suitable for freezing.

Belgian Eels

450 g (1 lb) eel, skinned
50 g (2 oz) butter or block
  margarine
1 small onion, skinned and
  sliced

450 g (1 lb) fresh spinach,
  washed and chopped
15 ml (1 tbsp) chopped fresh
  parsley
450 ml (¾ pint) white wine

salt and freshly ground
  pepper
30 ml (2 tbsp) lemon juice
3 egg yolks

SERVES 4

Cut the fish into 5 cm (2 inch) lengths. Melt the fat in a flameproof casserole and cook the onion and spinach for a few minutes, then add the eels, parsley, seasoning and wine. Cover and cook gently for about 20 minutes until the fish and spinach are tender. Mix together the lemon juice and egg yolks and stir into the wine liquid. Reheat to serving temperature but do not boil.

Not suitable for freezing.

Squid in Red Wine

1 kg (2 lb) squid
30 ml (2 tbsp) oil —
  preferably olive
1 large onion, skinned and
  sliced

juice of 1 lemon
2 stalks celery, trimmed and
  sliced
2 garlic cloves, skinned and
  crushed

15 ml (1 level tbsp) flour
450 ml (¾ pint) red wine
30 ml (2 tbsp) chopped fresh
  parsley

SERVES 4

Hold the body of the squid in one hand and pull off the tentacles and the contents of the body. Remove the small dark ink sacs. Cut off the head and discard. Peel off the skin and rinse well under cold running water. Cut the flesh into thin strips and leave to marinate in a bowl with the lemon juice and the oil for at least 30 minutes. Strain off the marinade and put in a flameproof casserole. Add the onion and celery and sauté for about 5 minutes, then add the garlic. Add the flour and cook for 2 minutes then add the red wine and the squid pieces. Bring to the boil and simmer for about 1¼ hours or until the squid is tender. Sprinkle with chopped parsley for serving.

Not suitable for freezing.

Scampi Provençale

1 kg (2 lb) shelled scampi
1 medium onion, skinned
  and finely sliced
1 garlic clove, skinned and
  crushed

30 ml (2 tbsp) olive oil
397-g (14-oz) can of
  tomatoes, drained
150 ml (¼ pint) dry white
  wine

1.25 ml (¼ level tsp) dried
  oregano
salt and freshly ground
  pepper
chopped parsley to garnish

SERVES 6

Thaw the scampi if using frozen ones and rinse them well under cold running water. Strain well and dry with kitchen paper. Heat the oil in a flameproof casserole and sauté the onion until soft. Add the crushed garlic and scampi, and sauté for 1 minute, stirring continuously.

Add the tomatoes, wine, oregano and seasoning. Bring to the boil and cover. Simmer for about 10 minutes, and check the seasoning. Sprinkle over chopped parsley and serve with boiled rice to soak up the juices.

Not suitable for freezing.

Fresh & Dried Vegetables

Vegetable dishes which are a meal in themselves are all too often considered the sole domain of the vegetarians. But there is no reason why, for a change, you should not serve a hearty bean and vegetable casserole as a main course – all the proteins are there just as in meat or fish, and you will be surprised at the way many of these dishes fill you up – for a fraction of the cost of meat. Of course they may also be used in smaller quantities to accompany meat, or many, like ratatouille, make an excellent starter. But try them on their own, perhaps with crusty bread to soak up the tasty juices, or a crisp green salad. Most of us like our vegetables lightly cooked with still a crunch to them, and it might seem strange to be recommending the long slow treatment that we give tough meat in a casserole. But many vegetables, particularly those available throughout the winter, respond beautifully to slow and gentle cooking, giving plenty of time for flavours to penetrate. Aubergines, tomatoes, onions, peppers, fennel, leeks, celery and courgettes impart a wonderful flavour to any casserole, and all the root vegetables – carrots, turnips, swedes or potatoes and celeriac, take time to absorb pungent spices or aromatic gravies, but the resulting dish is well worth the wait.

Of course meat need not be completely excluded from these vegetable casseroles – a bit of sausage, salami or bacon will often add a savoury touch which only complements the flavour. Cabbage leaves, peppers, tomatoes or onions can be stuffed with rice or meat mixtures, and left to simmer in the casserole.

Cooking Dried Vegetables

Dried vegetables – peas, beans, lentils or any pulses – are widely available in super-markets and wholefood shops, and some require long and gentle simmering before they are edible, so they are ideal subjects for the pot. They are full of protein, vitamins and minerals, so if cooked with fresh vegetables provide a good balanced meal.

All but lentils require soaking overnight in cold water before cooking, though if you make a late decision to include pulses in your menu, it is possible to give them a short hot soak, by covering them with a generous amount of cold water, bringing them to the boil, and allowing them to boil for a few minutes before leaving them to soak, covered, for at least an hour. Do be sure that you cook them for the specified time when using them in these recipes.

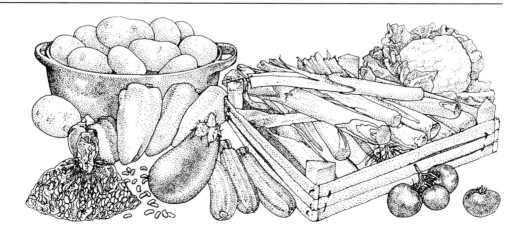

Spiced Ragout

450 g (1 lb) medium potatoes, peeled
225 g (½ lb) small onions, skinned and halved
50 g (2 oz) butter or margarine
5 ml (1 level tsp) chilli seasoning
30 ml (2 level tbsp) flour

5 ml (1 level tsp) ground cardamom
2.5 ml (½ level tsp) ground turmeric
2.5 ml (½ level tsp) ground coriander
397-g (14-oz) can tomatoes
1 garlic clove, skinned and crushed

300 ml (½ pint) chicken stock
150 ml (¼ pint) natural yogurt
salt and freshly ground pepper
8 eggs, hardboiled
chopped parsley to garnish

SERVES 4

Slice the potatoes into finger-size pieces.

Lightly brown the onions and potatoes in the hot fat in a large saucepan. Add the spices and flour and cook for 1 minute, stirring.

Add the tomatoes with their juice, garlic, stock, yogurt and seasoning and bring to the boil.

Cover and simmer gently for about 40 minutes; adjust the seasoning.

Shell the eggs and halve lengthwise; add to the sauce and leave over a low heat to get really hot.

Sprinkle with chopped parsley for serving.

Suitable for freezing. Freeze without the eggs. Reheat in the usual way and add eggs.

Braised Red Cabbage

900 g (2 lb) red cabbage
50 g (2 oz) butter or margarine
125 g (4 oz) streaky bacon rashers, rinded and chopped

15 ml (1 level tbsp) flour
1 medium onion, skinned and sliced
350 g (12 oz) cooking apples, peeled, cored and sliced
45 ml (3 tbsp) cider vinegar

20 ml (4 level tsp) granulated sugar
salt and freshly ground pepper

SERVES 4–6

Peel the outer damaged leaves off the cabbage and discard. Quarter the cabbage and then shred finely, removing the core. Blanch the cabbage in boiling water for 3 minutes, drain well in a colander. At this stage the cabbage will look blue. Melt the fat in a medium-sized flameproof casserole, add the bacon and cook for 5 minutes then stir in the flour and then add the cabbage, onion, apples, vinegar, sugar and seasoning together with 75 ml (5 tbsp) water.

Mix the ingredients well together, cover tightly, placing greased greaseproof paper under the lid.

Cook in the oven at 170°C (325°F) mark 3 for about 1½ hours or until the cabbage is quite tender.

Not suitable for freezing.

Dolmas

700 (1½ lb) green cabbage
15 ml (1 tbsp) vegetable oil
1 medium onion, skinned
    and chopped
450 g (1 lb) fresh minced
    lamb or beef

50 g (2 oz) long grain rice,
    cooked
60 ml (4 level tbsp) chutney
75 g (3 oz) raisins
5 ml (1 level tsp) salt
397-g (14-oz) can tomatoes

1 beef stock cube
15 ml (1 tbsp)
    Worcestershire sauce
pinch of paprika

SERVES 4

Separate 8–10 large, but not outside leaves from the cabbage and cut out the hard stem from the base of each. Wash the leaves in cold water, then blanch in boiling water for 2 minutes. Drain.

Discard the coarse stem from the remaining cabbage and shred the leaves finely; fry them with chopped onion in oil for 2 minutes. Add the lamb and cook gently for a further 10 minutes. Remove from the heat and add rice, chutney, raisins and salt.

Divide the mixture between the blanched cabbage leaves, then fold the leaves over to enclose the filling. Secure each with a cocktail stick.

Blend or sieve the tomatoes, then combine them with their juice, the stock cube, Worcestershire sauce and paprika.

Place stuffed cabbage leaves in an ovenproof dish and pour the sauce over them. Cover and cook at 190°C (375°F) mark 5 for about 45 minutes.

Not suitable for freezing.

Potato, Carrot and Onion Bourguignonne

25 g (1 oz) butter or
    margarine
15 ml (1 tbsp) vegetable oil
15 ml (1 level tbsp) demerara
    sugar
225 g (8 oz) carrots, peeled
    and sliced
15 ml (1 level tbsp) flour

225 g (8 oz) small onions,
    skinned
450 g (1 lb) small new
    potatoes, scrubbed and
    halved
125 g (4 oz) button
    mushrooms, wiped
150 ml (¼ pint) red wine

10 ml (2 level tsp) tomato
    purée
150 ml (¼ pint) beef stock
1 bayleaf
salt and freshly ground
    pepper
125 g (4 oz) Cheddar cheese,
    cubed

SERVES 2

Heat the butter and oil together in a flameproof casserole. Add the sugar, carrots, onions and potatoes, and cook stirring until vegetables begin to colour. Add the mushrooms, cook for a further minute.

Stir in the flour, scraping any sediment from the bottom of the pan. Add the red wine, tomato purée, stock, bayleaf and seasoning.

Cover tightly and cook in the oven at 190°C (375°F) mark 5 for about 1 hour. Add cheese cubes for last 10 minutes of cooking time to melt.

Remove bayleaf. Check seasoning and serve.

Not suitable for freezing.

Two Bean Vegetable Curry

125 g (4 oz) dried soya
   beans, soaked overnight
125 g (4 oz) dried black
   beans, soaked overnight
700 g (1½ lb) cauliflower
1 medium onion, skinned
½ green pepper, seeded
small piece fresh root ginger,
   peeled

450 g (1 lb) courgettes
30 ml (2 tbsp) vegetable oil
125 g (4 oz) button
   mushrooms, wiped
10 ml (2 level tsp) sugar
20 ml (4 level tsp) ground
   coriander
10 ml (2 level tsp) ground
   cumin

5 ml (1 level tsp) ground
   turmeric
15 ml (1 level tbsp) tomato
   purée
900 ml (1½ pint) chicken
   stock
salt and freshly ground
   pepper
30 ml (2 level tbsp) cornflour

SERVES 4

Drain the beans. Cook the soya beans in plenty of water; after 30 minutes add the black beans and cook for a further 1 hour.

Trim the cauliflower, divide into small florets; finely slice the onion and pepper; thickly slice the courgettes; crush or finely chop ginger. Lightly brown the onion and pepper in oil. Stir in whole mushrooms and courgettes; cook for 5 minutes. Add the ginger, sugar, coriander, cumin, turmeric, tomato purée and stock. Stir in the cauliflower and beans. Bring to the boil. Adjust seasoning, reduce heat, cover and simmer for about 20 minutes. Blend cornflour to a cream with cold water. Stir into the mixture; simmer, uncovered, for 5 minutes.

Not suitable for freezing.

Leeky Stew with a Nackerjack

This soup-cum-stew, abundant with fresh vegetables, is topped with a large dumpling known in South Devon as a nackerjack. A hearty one-pot meal that the tin miners used to enjoy on high-days and holidays.

450 g (1 lb) leeks, trimmed
350 g (¾ lb) potatoes, peeled
350 g (12 oz) lean bacon
900 ml (1½ pint) chicken
   stock

salt and freshly ground
   pepper

For the nackerjack
225 g (8 oz) self-raising flour

2.5 ml (½ level tsp) salt
100 g (4 oz) shredded suet
water to mix

SERVES 4

Halve or quarter the leeks, cut in 7.5-cm (3-inch) lengths and wash well. Cut the potatoes and bacon into fairly large pieces and place in a 2.3-litre (4-pint) ovenproof dish with the leeks, stock and seasoning. Cover and cook in the oven at 200°C (400°F) mark 6 for 1 hour.

Make the nackerjack, mixing all the ingredients to form a soft dough. Pat out on a floured surface to 2.5 cm (1 inch) thick. Place carefully on to the stew, cover, and return to the oven for about a further 20 minutes.

Not suitable for freezing.

Vegetable Couscous

Couscous, national dish of the North African countries, takes its name from a fine semolina made of wheat grain. Couscous is eaten in the same way as we eat rice, together with a cross between a robust broth and a stew, our version features a pleasing balance of mildly aromatic spices, although some local variations are far hotter and spicier and include chicken or meat, sometimes both. The dish is traditionally made in a couscousier — a large steamer. Buy the uncooked couscous and be sure to soak it properly for a light finish. If you do buy the part-cooked variety, all you need do is put the couscous in a heated serving dish, pour on enough boiling water just to cover, add 5 ml (1 level tsp) salt, stir quickly and cover with a lid. Leave to stand in a warm place for 10 minutes.

450 g (1 lb) couscous
400 ml (¾ pint) tepid water
225 g (8 oz) turnips, peeled and diced
1 red pepper, seeded and diced
1 green pepper, seeded and diced
2 medium onions, skinned and diced
2 carrots, trimmed and scrubbed and diced

4 courgettes, washed, trimmed and sliced into 1-cm (½-inch) slices
1 small cauliflower, trimmed, washed and divided into small florets
4 large tomatoes, skinned and chopped
2 garlic cloves, skinned and crushed
1.1 litres (2 pints) vegetable stock

salt and freshly ground pepper
225 g (8 oz) chick peas, soaked overnight
25 g (1 oz) blanched almonds
5 ml (1 level tsp) turmeric
10 ml (2 level tsp) paprika
2.5 ml (½ level tsp) ground coriander
75 g (3 oz) butter
100 g (4 oz) dried apricots, soaked overnight

SERVES 6 —————————————————— *Illustrated in colour opposite page 97*

Place the couscous in a large bowl with the water and leave to soak for 1 hour. Place the vegetables in a large saucepan with the garlic, stock, seasoning, chick peas, nuts and spices. Bring to the boil, cover and simmer for 30 minutes.

Drain the couscous grains and place them in a steamer on the saucepan over the vegetables. Cover and continue cooking for a further 40 minutes, then remove the steamer and cover the saucepan.

Place the couscous in a large mixing bowl. Melt the butter and beat it into the couscous with 50 ml (2 fl oz) salt water. Leave for 15 minutes. Drain and quarter the apricots, add them to the vegetables and simmer for 15 minutes. Stir the couscous well to remove any lumps and return it to the steamer over the simmering vegetables for 20 minutes, covered. Serve the vegetables and couscous separately in warm serving dishes.

Not suitable for freezing.

Black Beans in Rum

25 g (1 oz) butter
1 medium onion, skinned
    and finely sliced
50 g (2 oz) celery, finely
    diced

100 g (4 oz) carrot, peeled
    and diced
225 g (8 oz) black beans,
    soaked overnight
150 ml (¼ pint) dark rum

700 ml (1¼ pints) unseasoned
    beef stock
10 ml (2 level tsp) salt
freshly ground black pepper
soured cream to serve

SERVES 4

Melt the butter and sauté the vegetables to soften them a little.

Add the drained beans, stock, half the rum, and salt. Cover and simmer for about 1 hour or until the beans are tender and all the liquid is absorbed. Add the remaining rum and sprinkle liberally with black pepper before serving with well stirred soured cream.

Suitable for freezing. Freeze without soured cream. Reheat in the usual way and add soured cream.

Ratatouille

A classic vegetable dish to serve with grilled meats, alone as a starter or for supper with French bread.

30 ml (2 tbsp) vegetable oil
25 g (1 oz) butter
4 tomatoes, skinned and
    sliced
2 aubergines, sliced

1 small green pepper, seeded
    and sliced
2 onions, skinned and sliced
salt and freshly ground
    pepper

2 courgettes, sliced
1 garlic clove, skinned and
    crushed
cheese croûtes (optional)
    (see page 122)

SERVES 4

Heat the oil and butter in a flameproof casserole and add the prepared vegetables, seasoning and garlic. Stir well, cover tightly and cook in the oven at 180°C (350°F) mark 4 for 1–1¼ hours, until the vegetables are tender. Place the croûtes on top to serve.

Suitable for freezing. Reheat in the usual way. Add croûtes if wished.

Braised Leeks

8 medium leeks – about 900 g
    (2 lb) total weight
25 g (1 oz) butter or
    margarine

125 g (4 oz) rindless streaky
    bacon, chopped
150 ml (¼ pint) chicken stock
2 bayleaves

salt and freshly ground
    pepper
125 g (4 oz) Red Leicester
    cheese, grated

SERVES 4

Trim off and discard any coarse dark green leaves. Split the leeks open without cutting in half and wash to remove all grit. Melt the fat in a shallow flameproof casserole. Add the leeks and bacon and fry gently until golden. Stir in the stock with the bayleaves and seasoning and bring to the boil. Cover tightly and cook in the oven at 170°C (325°F) mark 3 for about 1 hour, or until the leeks are just tender. Sprinkle over the cheese and grill until bubbling.

Not suitable for freezing.

Ragout of Carrots

If you don't think vegetables on their own are enough for lunch or supper, you'll change your mind when you taste this medley. Serve it with rice.

1 kg (2½ lb) carrots	50 g (2 oz) raisins	5 ml (1 level tsp) salt
225 g (8 oz) baby onions, skinned	100 g (4 oz) butter	freshly ground pepper
225 g (8 oz) button mushrooms, wiped	150 ml (¼ pint) dry white wine	chopped parsley to garnish
	2.5 ml (½ level tsp) aniseed	

SERVES 4

Peel the carrots or scrape them if they are young. Cut into 5-cm (2-inch) lengths, or leave whole if small. Melt the butter in a flameproof casserole. Add the wine, vegetables, raisins, aniseed, salt and pepper. Bring to the boil, cover, reduce heat and simmer for 30–35 minutes until the vegetables are tender but not too soft. Remove the lid and open boil, stirring occasionally, until the liquid is reduced to a glaze. Garnish with chopped parsley and serve with rice.

Not suitable for freezing.

Boston Beans

275 g (10 oz) dried haricot or cannellini beans, soaked overnight	2 medium onions, skinned and chopped	30 ml (2 level tbsp) tomato purée
225 g (8 oz) fat salt belly of pork	5 ml (1 level tsp) dry mustard powder	10 ml (2 level tsp) dark brown sugar
15 ml (1 tbsp) vegetable oil	15 ml (1 tbsp) black treacle	300 ml (½ pint) chicken stock
	150 ml (¼ pint) tomato juice	

SERVES 4 ———————————————————— *Illustrated in colour opposite page 97*

Drain the beans and place in a pan of water. Bring to the boil and then boil for 25 minutes. Drain. Cut the pork into 2.5-cm (1-inch) cubes.

Fry the onion in the oil, ideally in a flameproof casserole.

Remove from the heat, add the pork and the remaining ingredients and stir well.

Bring to the boil and place the covered casserole in the oven at 140°C (275°F) mark 1. Cook for about 2½–3 hours, until the beans are tender and the sauce is the consistency of syrup. Stir from time to time to prevent sticking.

Not suitable for freezing.

Bean and Vegetable Stew

175 g (6 oz) cannellini beans, soaked overnight	100 g (4 oz) celery	2.5 ml (½ level tsp) dried thyme
700 ml (1¼ pints) seasoned chicken stock	1 medium onion, skinned	15 ml (1 level tbsp) cornflour
225 g (½ lb) courgettes	100 g (4 oz) red pepper, seeded	salt and freshly ground pepper
225 g (½ lb) aubergine	25 g (1 oz) butter	
	150 ml (¼ pint) dry cider	

SERVES 4–6

Drain the beans and place in a pan with the stock. Bring to the boil, cover and simmer for 45 minutes. The beans should be tender but still a little firm.

Trim and slice the vegetables. Melt the butter in a large deep flameproof casserole and sauté vegetables a few at a time until golden.

Add the vegetables to the beans with the stock. Add the cider and thyme, cover and simmer gently for about 15 minutes until the beans and vegetables are tender.

Blend cornflour to a cream with a little cold water and stir into the pan; bring to the boil, stirring. Cook until thickened. Adjust seasoning before serving.

Not suitable for freezing.

Lentils with Rice

225 g (8 oz) streaky bacon rashers, rinded	5 ml (1 level tsp) ground ginger	salt and freshly ground pepper
40 g (1½ oz) butter or margarine	275 g (10 oz) long grain rice	225 g (8 oz) frozen peas
5 ml (1 level tsp) turmeric	175 g (6 oz) red lentils	50 g (2 oz) blanched almonds
	1 litre (1¾ pints) chicken stock	

SERVES 4

Cut the bacon into small pieces. Heat 25 g (1 oz) fat in a shallow flameproof casserole and fry the bacon for 3 minutes. Add the turmeric and ginger and cook for a further minute. Add the rice and lentils and stir well to coat the grains. Add the stock and seasoning and cover tightly. Cook in the oven at 170°C (325°F) mark 3 for 50 minutes, then stir in the frozen peas. Re-cover and cook for about a further 10 minutes until the grains are tender and the liquid is absorbed.

Meanwhile fry the almonds in the remaining butter until golden and use to garnish the casserole.

Not suitable for freezing.

Bean and Aubergine Curry

225 g (8 oz) blackeye beans,
  soaked overnight
225 g (8 oz) aubergine
salt
225 g (8 oz) onion, skinned
  and sliced

25 g (1 oz) butter
2.5 ml (½ level tsp) ground
  ginger
2.5 ml (½ level tsp) turmeric
2.5 ml (½ level tsp) coriander
15 ml (1 level tbsp) flour

30 ml (2 level tbsp) curry
  paste
300 ml (½ pint) chicken stock
  or water

SERVES 4

Drain beans and cook in boiling water for about 50 minutes or until almost tender.

Trim and slice the aubergine, spread slices out on a plate and sprinkle with salt; leave to stand for 30 minutes. Wash in cold water and drain.

Sauté the onion in the butter to soften. Add the spices and curry paste. Cook gently, stirring, for 5 minutes. Stir in the flour, then gradually add the stock. Bring to the boil, then add the beans and aubergine.

Cover and simmer very gently for 15–20 minutes until the aubergine is tender. Adjust the seasoning and serve with rice.

Suitable for freezing. Reheat in the usual way.

Root Vegetable Hot Pot

175 g (6 oz) carrot, peeled
  and thinly sliced
100 g (4 oz) onion, skinned
  and thinly sliced
50 g (2 oz) celery, trimmed,
  washed and thinly sliced

100 g (4 oz) swede, peeled
  and thinly sliced
15 ml (1 level tbsp) cornflour
300 ml (½ pint) vegetable,
  chicken or beef stock
bouquet garni

salt and freshly ground
  pepper
212-g (7½-oz) can butter
  beans
100 g (4 oz) frozen peas

SERVES 4

Layer the vegetables in a 2.3-litre (4-pint) casserole.

Blend the cornflour with a little of the stock, add the remainder and put in the casserole with the bouquet garni and seasonings.

Cover and bake in the oven at 180°C (350°F) mark 4 for 1 hour.

Add the drained beans and peas and return to the oven for about 20 minutes.

Check the seasoning, remove bouquet garni and serve with crusty bread or baked jacket potatoes.

Suitable for freezing. Reheat in the usual way.

Toppings, Stocks & Flavourings

Toppings

Your repertoire of casseroles can be greatly extended by the addition of a variety of interesting toppings, many of which can be made in quantity, then frozen. When a recipe specifies, for example, 100 g (4 oz) pastry, this means pastry made using 100 g (4 oz) flour, with the other ingredients in proportion.

Shortcrust Pastry

For shortcrust pastry, you use half the quantity of fat to flour. Therefore, for a recipe using quantities of shortcrust pastry other than 225 g (8 oz) simply use half the quantity of fat to flour weight specified.

225 g (8 oz) flour
pinch of salt

50 g (2 oz) butter or block margarine
50 g (2 oz) lard

Mix the flour and salt together in a bowl. Cut the fat into small pieces and add to the flour. Lightly rub in the fats until the mixture resembles fine breadcrumbs. Add 30–45 ml (2–3 tbsp) chilled water evenly over the surface and stir in until the mixture begins to stick together in large lumps. With one hand, collect the mixture together to form a ball. Knead lightly for a few seconds to give a firm, smooth dough. Do not over-handle the dough. The pastry can be used straight away, but it is better if allowed to 'rest' for about 30 minutes wrapped in foil or cling film in the refrigerator. Roll out the pastry on a lightly floured surface and use as required. The ideal thickness is usually about 0.3 cm ($\frac{1}{8}$ inch). Do not pull or stretch the pastry. When cooking shortcrust pastry, the usual oven temperature is 200–220°C (400–425°F) mark 6–7.

To freeze: Both baked and unbaked shortcrust pastry freeze well. Thaw unbaked dough at room temperature before unwrapping, but rolled out pastry may be cooked from frozen, allowing a little extra time.

Choux Pastry

This is a light, airy, easy to make pastry. It can be added as a topping to any oven-cooked casserole with lots of liquid.

50 g (2 oz) butter or block
   margarine
150 ml ($\frac{1}{4}$ pint) water
65 g ($2\frac{1}{2}$ oz) plain flour, sifted

2 eggs, lightly beaten (see
   method)
15 ml (1 tbsp) chopped fresh
   parsley

SERVES 4

Put the fat and water together in a saucepan, heat gently until the fat has melted, then bring to the boil. Remove the pan from the heat. Tip all the flour at once into the hot liquid. Beat thoroughly with a wooden spoon, then return the pan to the heat. Continue beating the mixture until it is smooth and forms a ball in the centre of the pan. (Take care not to over-beat or the mixture will become fatty.) Remove from the heat and leave the mixture to cool for a minute or two. Beat in the eggs a little at a time, adding only just enough to give a piping consistency. (Use size 4 eggs if beating by hand and size 2 eggs when using an electric mixer.) It is important to beat the mixture vigorously at this stage to trap in as much air as possible until the mixture develops a sheen. A hand-held mixer is ideal. Beat in the parsley. Spoon or pipe the mixture on top of a casserole about 45 minutes before the end of the cooking time. Bake in the oven, uncovered, at 200°C (400°F) mark 6 until choux is risen and golden brown.

Rough Puff Pastry

Similar in appearance and texture to puff pastry, rough puff pastry makes a good alternative as it is quicker and easier to make.

225 g (8 oz) plain flour
pinch of salt
75 g (3 oz) butter or block margarine
75 g (3 oz) lard

about 150 ml ($\frac{1}{4}$ pint) cold
   water and a squeeze of
   lemon juice
beaten egg to glaze

Mix the flour and salt together in a bowl. Cut the fat (which should be quite firm) into cubes about 2 cm ($\frac{3}{4}$ inch) across. Stir the fat into the flour without breaking up the pieces. Add enough water and lemon juice to mix to a fairly stiff dough. On a lightly floured surface, roll out into an oblong three times as long as it is wide. Fold the bottom third up and the top third down, then turn the pastry so that the folded edges are at the sides. Seal the ends of the pastry by pressing lightly with a rolling pin. Repeat this rolling and folding process three more times, turning the dough so that the folded edge is on the left hand side each time. Wrap the pastry in greaseproof paper and leave to 'rest' in the refrigerator or a cool place for about 30 minutes before using. Roll out the pastry on a lightly floured surface to 0.3 cm ($\frac{1}{8}$ inch) thick and use as required. Brush with beaten egg before baking. The usual oven temperature is 220°C (425°F) mark 7.

To freeze: Pack in freezer cling film or foil. Thaw at room temperature for $1\frac{1}{2}$–2 hours.

Puff Pastry

The richest of all the pastries, puff gives the most even rising, the most flaky effect and the crispest texture, but because of the time it takes, most people make it only occasionally. It requires very careful handling and whenever possible should be made the day before it is to be used, so that it has time to become firm and cool before it is shaped and baked. Bought puff pastry, either chilled or frozen, is very satisfactory, but remember to roll it out to only a maximum thickness of 0.3 cm ($\frac{1}{8}$ inch), as it rises very well. One pound of puff pastry is equivalent to two 368-g (13-oz) packets of frozen.

450 g (1 lb) strong plain flour
pinch of salt
450 g (1 lb) butter

300 ml ($\frac{1}{2}$ pint) iced water
15 ml (1 tbsp) lemon juice
beaten egg to glaze

Mix the flour and salt together in a bowl. Cut off 50 g (2 oz) of butter and pat the remaining butter with a rolling pin to a slab 2 cm ($\frac{3}{4}$ inch) thick. Rub the 50 g (2 oz) of butter into the flour. Stir in enough water and lemon juice to make a soft, elastic dough. Knead the dough until smooth and shape into a round. Cut through half the depth in the shape of a cross. Open out the flaps to form a star. Roll out, keeping the centre four times as thick as the flaps. Place the slab of butter in the centre of the dough and fold over the flaps, envelope-style. Press gently with a rolling pin and roll out into a rectangle measuring about 40 × 20 cm (16 × 8 inch). Fold the bottom third up and the top third down, keeping the edges straight. Seal the edges by pressing with the rolling pin. Wrap the pastry in greaseproof paper and leave in the refrigerator to 'rest' for 30 minutes. Put the pastry on a lightly floured working surface with the folded edges to the sides and repeat the rolling, folding and resting sequence five times. After the final resting, roll out the pastry on a lightly floured surface and shape as required. Brush with beaten egg before baking. The usual oven temperature is 230°C (450°F) mark 8.

To freeze: Pack in freezer cling film or foil in amounts that are practical to thaw and use. Thaw at room temperature for $1\frac{1}{2}$–2 hours.

Suetcrust Pastry

This pastry may be used for a lid of a casserole or for dumplings. Suetcrust pastry is quick and easy to make, and can be boiled or baked.

225 g (8 oz) self-raising flour
2.5 ml ($\frac{1}{2}$ level tsp) salt

100 g (4 oz) shredded suet
about 150 ml ($\frac{1}{4}$ pint) cold water

Mix the flour, salt and suet together in a bowl. Stir in enough cold water to give a light, elastic dough. Knead very gently until smooth. Roll or pat out on a lightly floured surface to 2.5 cm (1 inch) thick. Place carefully on top of a casserole 20–25 minutes before the end of the cooking time. Simmer on top of the cooker or bake in the oven at 200°C (400°F) mark 6 unless otherwise stated.

Not suitable for freezing.

Swimmers

Dumplings weren't always made from suet. In East Anglia in Victorian times, housewives used to pinch off small pieces of risen yeast dough from the bowl beside the hearth, and boil them in water. These light puffy balls were – and are – very good floated in the rich gravy of a 'sloppy' stew.

125 g (4 oz) strong plain
    flour
2.5 ml (½ level tsp) salt
75 ml (3 fl oz) warm water

15 g (½ oz) fresh yeast or
5 ml (1 level tsp) dried
yeast and 2.5 ml (½ level
tsp) sugar

MAKES 8

Sieve the flour and salt into a bowl. If using fresh yeast, blend with the water or if using dried yeast, add it with the sugar to the warm water and leave in a warm place for about 15 minutes until frothy. Make a well in the centre of the bowl and add the yeast liquid. Mix the dough until it leaves the sides of the bowl. Turn on to a floured surface and knead well for 10 minutes until elastic. Place in a bowl and cover with a clean cloth. Leave to rise in a warm place for about 1 hour until doubled in size. Divide the risen dough into eight pieces and gently form into balls. Place on the top of the casserole ingredients about 30 minutes before cooking time is complete. Cover the casserole again and simmer gently on top of the cooker or bake in the oven at 200°C (400°F) mark 6 until the swimmers swell and are cooked through.

Cobblers

225 g (8 oz) self-raising flour
30 ml (2 tbsp) chopped fresh
    parsley (optional)

1.25 ml (¼ level tsp) salt
about 150 ml (¼ pint) milk

MAKES ABOUT 12

Place the flour and salt into a bowl. Rub in the fat until the mixture resembles fine breadcrumbs. Add the parsley if used. Make a well in the centre and add sufficient milk to give a soft but manageable dough. Turn out on to a lightly floured surface, knead lightly and roll out the dough to 1 cm (½ inch) thickness. Cut out rounds using a 4-cm (1½-inch) plain cutter. Brush with milk and arrange overlapping around the edge of the casserole. Bake in the oven at 220°C (425°F) mark 7 for 10–15 minutes until the topping is golden brown.

Croûtons

Fried: Cut bread into 0.5–1-cm (¼–½-inch) cubes and fry quickly in deep or shallow oil until crisp and golden.

Toasted: Cut slices of toast into 0.5–1-cm (¼–½-inch) dice. Serve croûtons separately or sprinkle them over a casserole.

Dumplings

100 g (4 oz) suetcrust pastry
(see page 119)

freshly chopped or dried
herbs (optional)

salt and freshly ground
pepper

MAKES 8

Make the pastry, adding herbs and seasoning to the dry mix. Divide the pastry into eight equal pieces and shape into balls.

Add the dumplings to a casserole about 15–25 minutes before cooking is complete, then reduce the heat and cover the casserole. Simmer gently on top of the cooker or bake in the oven at 200°C (400°F) mark 6 unless otherwise stated until the dumplings swell. Do not allow the liquid to boil or the dumplings will disintegrate.

Fried Crumbs

50–100 g (2–4 oz) fresh
breadcrumbs
25 g (1 oz) butter

Fry the breadcrumbs in the butter until golden brown. Stir from time to time to ensure even browning.

Pastry Puffs

212-g (7-oz) packet puff
pastry, thawed

beaten egg to glaze
snipped parsley to garnish

Thinly roll out the pastry on a lightly floured surface. Stamp out different sized fluted rounds and make a small hole in centre of each. Brush with beaten egg and bake in the oven at 220°C (425°F) mark 7 for about 15 minutes until golden brown and risen. Scatter the pastry rounds over a casserole and garnish dish with snipped parsley.

Swede and Potato Lattice

350 g (12 oz) potato, peeled
350 g (12 oz) swede, peeled
25 g (1 oz) butter or
margarine

salt and freshly ground
pepper
25 g (1 oz) Cheddar cheese,
grated

Cook the potato and swede in salted water until tender. Drain very well, push through a mouli or wire sieve. Beat in the fat, then season. Pipe or spoon over a casserole, sprinkle the cheese on top and flash under the grill to brown.

Cheese Croûtes

100 g (4 oz) Cheddar cheese,
   grated
slices of French bread

Sprinkle the cheese on top of the slices of French bread. Grill until golden brown.

Savoury Crumbs

350 g (12 oz) fresh
   breadcrumbs
2.5 ml (½ level tsp) salt
2.5 ml (½ level tsp) cayenne pepper

75 g (3 oz) butter or block
   margarine
60 ml (4 tbsp) chopped fresh
   parsley

Put the breadcrumbs in a large bowl. Add the seasonings. Rub in the fat. Add the parsley and stir well. Use as a savoury topping sprinkled over a casserole. Brown under the grill.

To freeze: Pack in a large plastic bag. The crumbs stay free flowing, so you can use as much as you need.

Bacon Thatch

125 g (4 oz) wide streaky
   bacon, rinded

On a wooden board, stretch each rasher of bacon using the back of a knife and divide into two. Concertina by threading on to skewers. Place on a flat tin and bake alongside casserole until crisp. Arrange over the top of a casserole.

Savoury Crumble

This is particularly suitable for casseroles cooked with little liquid and for topping vegetable casseroles.

175 g (6 oz) flour
5 ml (1 tsp) chopped fresh
   herbs or 2.5 ml (½ tsp)
   dried mixed herbs

75 g (3 oz) butter or block
   margarine
salt and freshly ground
   pepper

Place the flour in a bowl and rub in the fat until the mixture resembles fine breadcrumbs. Stir in the herbs and seasonings. Sprinkle the mixture on top of a casserole and bake in the oven at 400°C (200°F) mark 6 for about 30 minutes until golden brown.

Golden Onions

40 g (1½ oz) butter or
  margarine
1 medium onion, skinned
  and sliced into rings

40 g (1½ oz) fresh
  breadcrumbs
1 small garlic clove, skinned
  and crushed

Melt the fat in a pan and fry the onion with the breadcrumbs until golden. Stir in the garlic. Spoon over casserole.

Forcemeat Balls

125 g (4 oz) streaky bacon,
  rinded and finely chopped
1 small onion, skinned and
  finely chopped
1 egg, beaten

25 g (1 oz) butter, margarine
  or shredded suet
30 ml (2 level tbsp) chopped
  fresh herbs or 10 ml
  (2 level tsp) dried herbs

125 g (4 oz) fresh
  breadcrumbs
salt and freshly ground
  pepper

MAKES 6

Fry the bacon in its own fat until soft. Add the onion and fry until golden. Turn into a bowl and beat in the fat. Stir in the breadcrumbs, herbs and seasonings. Bind the mixture with the beaten egg and shape into six even-sized balls. Place them between the meat in a casserole, cover and cook in the oven at 190°C (375°F) mark 5 for 30 minutes.

Stocks

All your casseroles will benefit from the basis of a good home-made stock. There is usually something in the refrigerator which will help the flavour of a stock – a carcass, giblets or scraps of meat and vegetables. Butchers are often willing to give away a few bones which will enormously enhance the flavour of your stock, and make the resulting casserole even more delicious.

Basic Bone Stock

900 g (2 lb) meat bones,
  fresh or from cooked meat
cold water
2 onions

2 sticks celery
2 carrots
5 ml (1 level tsp) salt
3 peppercorns

bouquet garni or sprig of
  parsley and thyme,
  bayleaf, blade of
  mace, etc.

MAKES ABOUT 1.1 LITRES (2 PINTS)

Wash the bones and chop them up. If using a pressure cooker add 1.4 litres (2½ pints) water, bring to the boil and skim off any scum. Add roughly chopped vegetables, salt, peppercorns and herbs. Bring to high (15-lb) pressure and cook for 1–1¼ hours. If you are using marrow bones, increase the water to 1.7 litres (3 pints) and cook for 2 hours. Reduce pressure at room temperature.

In an ordinary pan use 2 litres (3½ pints) water. After skimming, add vegetables, etc, and simmer, well covered, for 5–6 hours. Strain the stock and, when cold, remove all traces of fat.

White Stock

900 g (2 lb) knuckle of veal,
  chopped
2.3 litres (4 pints) cold water

little lemon juice
1 onion, skinned and sliced
2 carrots, peeled and sliced

bouquet garni
5 ml (1 level tsp) salt

Put the bones in a large pan, add the water and lemon juice, bring to the boil and remove any scum that rises. Add the vegetables, bouquet garni and salt, reboil, cover and simmer for 5–6 hours. Strain and when cold remove any fat. Makes about 1.7 litres (3 pints).

Fish Stock

1 fish head or fish bones and
  trimmings
cold water

salt
bouquet garni
1 onion, skinned and sliced

Clean the head or wash the fish trimmings. Put in a saucepan, cover with water, add some salt, bring to the boil and skim. Reduce the heat and add the bouquet garni and onion. Cover, simmer for 20 minutes and strain. Use on the same day, or store in the refrigerator for not more than 2 days.

Brown Stock

450 g (1 lb) marrow bone or
   knuckle of veal, chopped
450 g (1 lb) shin of beef, cut
   into pieces

1.7 litres (3 pints) water
bouquet garni
1 medium onion, skinned
   and sliced

1 carrot, peeled and sliced
1 stick celery, sliced
2.5 ml (½ level tsp) salt

MAKES ABOUT 1.4 LITRES (2½ PINTS)

To give a good flavour and colour, brown the bones and meat in the oven (exact temperature not important) before using them. Put in a pan with the water, herbs, vegetables and salt, bring to the boil, skim and simmer covered for 5–6 hours. Pressure cook on high (15-lb) pressure as for basic bone stock, using 1.4 litres (2½ pints) water. Strain the stock and, when cold, remove all traces of fat.

Note For a more economical brown stock, use 900 g (2 lb) bones, omit the shin of beef and fry the onion until well browned.

Chicken Stock

MAKES 1.1–1.4 LITRES (2–2½ PINTS)

Break down the carcass and bones of a carved roast chicken and include any skin, chicken scraps, etc. Put in a pan with 1.4–1.7 litres (2½–3 pints) water, flavouring vegetables and herbs if you wish. Bring to the boil, skim and simmer, covered for 3 hours. Pressure cook at high (15-lb) for 45–60 minutes. Strain the stock and, when cold, remove all traces of fat.

Traditional Bouquet Garni

1 bayleaf
1 sprig of parsley

1 sprig of thyme
few peppercorns

Tie in a small piece of leek leaf or muslin. You can, of course, choose other herbs or include some dried mixed herbs.

Bouquet Garni (using dried herbs)

1 small bayleaf
pinch of dried mixed herbs
6 peppercorns

1 clove
pinch of dried parsley

Tie the herbs together in a small square of muslin with string or cotton, leaving a long end free to tie the bouquet garni to the handle of the pan.

Index